Medium

Medium

Lee Dunn

Refer to the disclaimer on page 289.

A special thanks to Claire, Liam and Madison.

You accept me for who I am.
You accept the long hours that I work.
You accept that I'll never be a millionaire.

Your love, support and patience is enduring.

Medium [Mee-dee-*uh*m]; a person who practices purported communication between spirits of the dead and living human beings.

CONTENTS

FOREWORD

"The soul is immortal, but many people don't realise their spiritual potential within."

Well, here we are. A massive thanks for buying this book. I've wanted to write it for a long time, but I've never really had the time to do it. Life has a habit of throwing things at us and some things just need to wait for another day. I've played around with various manuscripts for several years but the timing just hasn't been right. I've written many academic papers and published other works but this is the first time that I've attempted to collate my experiences and thoughts regarding mediumship. It's really about me and that's a scary thought!

I'm guessing that you're interested in mediumship and spirituality, otherwise you wouldn't be reading this book. It's also possible that you know me personally or that you're simply interested in what I have to say. If that's the case, I'm truly flattered in the thought that you've picked up my book. And if you've picked it up by *chance* rather than through *choice*, then perhaps there's a reason for that.

I'm going to warn you, now. This book is not scientific. It's not based on academic research or any evidence other than my own meandering experiential learning. It *is* factual as far as my experiences are concerned and everything that I present to you is real. It happened as I've described, but I have no way of proving it to you other than through my ramblings and through a few photographs scattered amongst the pages. You'll just need to take me at my word. A few of you may have been with me along the way and will remember the incidents that I describe. I've changed some names to protect people and their identities.

You'll also find some reflections at the end of each chapter, designed to help you raise your own awareness of spirit. It's *Get Your Sh*t Together* and *The Life-Changing Magic of Not Giving a F**k* all over again, both wonderful books written by Sarah Knight; highly recommended should you feel the need to get your life back on track. The main difference between her writing and mine, being that I hardly swear (well not often!) and I'm more interested in spirituality than practical steps towards self-efficacy.

So, if you're here to collate evidence about the paranormal, you'll be disappointed. BUT if you're here because you seek comfort in the knowledge that spirit exists, or you're trying to understand your own experiences, or because you want to understand the meaning of life, then I'll do my best to help you.

So, where to start?

The soul is immortal, but many people don't realise their spiritual potential within. We each have an awareness so profound that it could change your life in ways that you cannot possibly imagine. You're only a few steps away from the changes that you need, yet many of us do nothing about it.

Why is that?

There are many reasons why people don't embrace their spirituality. It can feel taboo at times. It may be for religious reasons or because they're sceptical. They may be worried about what other people may think or say. Perhaps they're afraid to open to spirit or they may have had frightening experiences that they can't easily explain.

We're often negative or indifferent to the things that scare us or to the things that we don't understand. That's human nature.

I get all of this.

It's a deeply personal thing and our beliefs, values and epistemologies define who we are. You are the architect of your own life and you need to remember that if you're working with other people, it's important not to dismiss their beliefs simply because they don't marry with yours. I've been caught out many times and trust me, it's often easier to just smile and nod your head politely, even if you disagree. It's very likely that you'll read this book and that you'll disagree with some of the things that I say. That's fine. I wouldn't expect anything less from you. One of my aims in writing this is to challenge your thinking and open up new possibilities.

If you want to take the next step and develop your

Visiting the ruins of Glenluce Abbey, Scotland (2019).

own spiritual awareness in a safe, nurturing environment, I'll provide you with guidance and advice throughout this book. I speak and write about life and being human and figuring things out along the way, with honest examples of the things that I've experienced and learned over the past 40 years. I'm certainly not the best or only medium that you may encounter, but my spiritualism is underpinned by honesty, integrity and mediumship from the heart.

These are my memoirs.

Love and light to you!

Lee.

END OF CHAPTER REFLECTION

Consider your own spiritual awareness. If you place yourself on a scale of 1 to 10 (10 is very spiritual), where would you position yourself? Why have you given yourself this score?

Not Spiritual   **Very Spiritual**

When you've finished reading this book, come back to the scale and determine if you've scored yourself correctly. This book will not make you more or less spiritual, as this is something that only comes from within you. It *will* shift your perception on spirituality, mediumship and what it means to be a spiritual being living a human experience. Watch out for more end of chapter reflections as these are designed to help raise your awareness of spirit.

SPOOKY ENCOUNTERS

"My physical encounters with ghostly apparitions and spirit tend to be brief."

The scream filled the night. It sounded like a banshee out for blood. My heart was racing and I knew right away what it meant. Spirit had a habit of appearing when I least expected. Despite being only 11 years old, I already knew this to be true.

Here I was messing around with my mate and without warning, I'm face-to-face with an elderly man out of time. The scream had come from outside, the source a child playing somewhere in the nearby vicinity. It wasn't ghostly and it may have been symbolic at the time, but I was more concerned about the sixty-something gentleman who was pointing at me from across the loft with a grim expression on his pale face.

This was not good. Not good at all.

I was inside an abandoned building. It was one of those old limestone built properties that had three levels, the top floor being the loft area. It was pretty big and several years later would be purchased by a property developer and turned into luxury homes. I can't name the building or tell you it's location as people now live there. I've often wondered if the old man was still haunting that building. Out the back, there was a single story extension. Part of the roof had collapsed and it was pretty easy for a nimble boy to climb onto the bins, hoist himself onto the flat roof and drop down inside the kitchen area. My mate, Robert gave me a punt up onto a bin to make life easier and a few minutes later I was inside.

There were dishes and cutlery items scattered around the counters. I don't know the history of the building but at some point it had obviously been a youth center or a place for kids to hang out. Each room seemed to be themed differently and there were many rooms. It was a bit like walking through a giant fun house in a long forgotten amusement park. The smell of damp and the taste of disturbed dust hung in the air as my feet kicked at the flooring, punctuated by peeling wallpaper, fading paint and the odd spider lurking in the corner of the room, scuttling along the skirting board.

"Can you see anything?" Robert asked.

I turned back and shouted back to him, only to see him peering inside from the collapsed roof.

"Aye, there's loads of clothes and stuff." I stepped over what appeared to be a pile of dressing gowns and stage production items.

"Try and get something and bring it back," Robert pleaded.

I told him that I would and I ventured deeper into the building. It didn't take long to realise that the atmosphere was changing. It was much cooler inside, where the sunlight was unable to penetrate the darkness through the windows, which had been boarded up with sheets of plywood. The odd beam of light managed to seep through the laminated boards where the damp peeled at their corners, illustrating the dust as I moved around. I carried on and went up the stairs, hearing Robert shouting to me again. I couldn't make out what he was saying so I decided to ignore him. On the upper level, I encountered pretty much the same. Rooms were littered with toys and children's books. One large room held my interest. It looked as though it had been used as a gym or an open area for games. Beanbags sat covered in mould and the gymnastics equipment looked sad, mounted to the wooden floorboards and forgotten for many years.

Adjacent to this room was an odd thing. I wasn't quite sure what to make of it. Half way up the wall was a hidden door. Or at least it had been hidden at some point, sealed up and covered by flower patterned wallpaper. Now, it lay open and I could see another set of stairs leading from the entrance and curving upwards out of sight. I had no idea why this would have been covered up, but my heart was beating quickly and the hairs on my arms started to stand on end. Goosebumps appeared on my exposed skin and I knew exactly what that meant.

I felt drawn upwards. I can't really explain this feeling. I've experienced it for many years and I now refer to it as psychic magnetism. It's a pull, or the overwhelming feeling that I need to move into a space, though the reason often eludes me.

I approached the door and noted the slight curvature in the steps as they moved upwards and out of sight. They were narrow and the steps themselves shallow. I gripped the frame and pulled myself up onto the ledge and then climbed to the third level. At the top, I found myself in the loft. It was a large open space that spanned the entire footprint of the building. The roof supports and the beams were visible and the bare floorboards were saturated in dust. I suspected that it was primarily used for storage at one point and then boarded up to keep people out. Toys and other items were scattered about. It didn't look very safe and part of the flooring was rotten were a leak in the slate tiled roof had allowed water to ingress.

That was when I saw him. He wasn't there a minute ago. But there he was now and I knew that he wasn't happy. His soul was in reflection (more about that later) and he was back to consider that point in his life. Pointing at me, his mouth opened as if he was going to speak and then he changed his mind, snapped it shut again and stood glaring at me.

My instincts told me to get out, but the episode didn't last long and then he was gone. I'd already experienced a few spooky encounters during my early childhood and this one didn't startle me or scare me in any way. This man was not threatening, though I didn't really want to hang around and wait for him to return. I knew he could try and interact physically, but that he had little chance of doing so. It takes a lot of energy for them to manifest into something that could do any physical harm and I didn't feel at risk.

I'd been in the building now for around ten minutes and I could hear muffled voices outside. The lack of insulation and the hole in the roof must have allowed the voices to carry upwards. It sounded like Robert was becoming agitated.

Looking around, I discovered a small, red plastic case with a microscope and chemistry items in it. I lifted it and proceeded back the way I had come, expecting my new mate to follow me. I glanced back and luckily he wasn't behind me, his anticipated icy cold hand reaching for the nape of my neck. As I moved back to the ground floor, I realised that Robert's voice was carrying from where I'd left him, but that he had been joined by an adult. I didn't recognise the voice.

Back in the kitchen, I said goodbye to the spirit man and jumped up onto the counter top. Grabbing the fallen timbers, I pulled myself up and back outside onto the roof, carrying my new chemistry set as I went.

"You," the man shouted at me. "Out here, now!"

I looked down to see a man in a black suit, white shirt and yellow tie. Robert shrugged at me, trying not to laugh. He thought this was amusing, even if a look of panic flashed through his eyes as they made contact with mine.

"You shouldn't be in there," the man said. "This is a dangerous building and you could end up hurt."

I decided that he was annoyed, but not angry. So I made up a story that we'd been walking along the street and some bigger boys had grabbed my chemistry set (which I now hugged to my chest) and they had thrown it in through the opening in the roof.

He eyed me with suspicion and I don't think he believed my story. He spent a few more minutes mouthing off at us, telling us to do one and not to come back.

I never mentioned the spirit man to Robert. We moved away quickly and started to walk home, considering what experiments we could do with our new science kit. It would be another five years before I would tell my friends that I could see the spirits of the dead.

* * *

I've actually lost count on the number of spooky encounters that I've experienced over the years. And by spooky, I don't just mean scary, but the type of encounters that fill the mind with wonder and awe. Until more recently, I've always avoided places which come with a reputation as being 'haunted'. When you read more, you'll see why. There is too much to tell you, so I'll account to you my more memorable experiences, with the intention of illustrating a timeline of sorts. I've also included a few memories provided by others who have witnessed my interactions with spirit, or where they themselves have had similar incidents to me.

I was born in Ormskirk, England in 1979. One of four children, I lived with my parents and my siblings, two older brothers and a younger sister. My grandparents lived in Leicester, England. When I was a child, I lived near Manchester and only a few hours along the M6 motorway, so we would regularly visit at the weekend. It was during one of our visits, when I clearly remember meeting spirit for the first time. I was very young, perhaps only a few years old, but the memory is vivid.

It was a Saturday afternoon. I know that because we had a regular routine. We would drive down to Oadby on the Friday night, planning to stay with my grandmother. We'd then relax on the Saturday morning (occasionally taking in a Leicester City FC game) and then on the Saturday afternoon we'd walk from the house to the village so that we could have a look around the shops.

Usually, we'd also visit my other grandmother, who lived in a nearby village called Thurnby Lodge. The Saturday evening was reserved for an obligatory visit to the Fish and Chip shop followed by some TV (*Noel's House Party*, *The Generation Game* and that sort of thing). There were always minor changes to the weekend schedule and I'd often play with my sister in the huge back garden, racing up and down the lawn and around the fruit trees on our beloved go cart, or throwing a few darts under the carport. The wooden doors looked like they had woodworm with all the holes we'd made over the years.

Sometimes, on the way to the shops we would walk through the local cemetery to pay our respects to those who had passed to the Higher Side of Life. It was a sunny, Saturday morning around 1983 as we cut through the cemetery, a path would lead a visitor from one side to the other and it would bring you out next to the shops. I remember the gate at the back of the cemetery and the water tap used by visitors to breathe life back into the graveside flowers. I used to enjoy visiting the pet shop in particular. Back in those days, they had various animals on display, including puppies, cats and rabbits as well as birds and small rodents. It was a real pet shop in the broadest sense and it was a favourite for many children.

The pet shop in Oadby, Leicester. I was a regular visitor during the 1980s.

As we neared the shop, the path would wind through a small street lined with bungalows. One of these had yellow painted woodwork. My grandmother knew the lady in residence and wanted to visit, as she wished to express her sorrow at the recent passing of her father. As we entered the house,

I noted to my right a front lounge area. The patterned carpet was well worn and there was a smell of home baking. In the lounge, I saw a hospital bed, on which sat an elderly gentlemen, equipped with an oxygen mask which was fed from a green tank sitting on the floor. He removed his mask and smiled at me as we went past the doorway and into the kitchen. It is here where my grandmother sat to chat with her friend. I didn't think too much about it at the time, until I later found out many years later that the elderly gentlemen had already passed over and the spirit that I had seen was her late father.

It was a good few years before I experienced anything else. Or at least, from which I can recollect any incident in sufficient detail to write about it here.

I was around eight years old in 1987, when I met George. I'd been out with my brothers. The house that we lived in was located near fields, accessible by a pathway known locally as the 'Green Bridge' because it was painted green. I'd play here with my friends, in a field that we called 'The Ferny'. It was essentially a large green belt with vast farmland and many ferns growing in the disused sections. It extended a good few miles down towards the M6 Motorway near Junction 27. Now the trouble with these ferns was that they tended to grow quite tall. For a smallish, eight year old, it was very easy to get lost. And that's exactly what happened to me. I managed, in a mild panic, to find my way out of The Ferny and into a neighboring field. I knew my brothers would be close as they had built a hay jump with their friends (it was perfectly acceptable back in those days to accumulate hay and straw from the failed bundles collated by the farmer).

Without warning, a man appeared at my side. He introduced himself as George and he was dressed in an old fashioned policeman's uniform, complete with trim hat and shiny silver buttons. He told me that he knew I was lost and that he would help me. He walked with me for a while and then pointed to a distant tree line. He told me that my brothers were 'over there'. I thanked him and he was gone.

To this day, I have no idea where he appeared from or where he went afterwards, but he was correct. I found my brothers and their friends and was able to make my way home. On telling my story to my parents a few years ago, I learned that my father once had a Great Uncle named George, who had been a policeman when he was alive. He had died on 27th October, 1986 aged 71. Could this have been the wayward spirit who stepped in to help me that day? Incidentally, my wife was born on 27th October. Life is full of these little synchronicities.

I had other experiences after that. We'd moved from the Shevington area to Leigh by this time. One of my teachers from my new school had passed away from cancer. She was extremely popular and when all the kids at school were told, I remember crying my eyes out with just about everyone else who could muster around the back of the bike sheds. The school bullies cried with the people they routinely bullied for death does not discriminate. My teacher had died shortly before Christmas and she had purchased a present for every child in the class as her final gift to us. I received a *Bravestar* gun, a blue plastic toy which wasn't politically correct, but was hugely satisfying. I'm sure I saw her that day, watching us and smiling from a distance as we were handed our gifts by the headteacher.

My first experience with something sinister was when I was around 10 years old and shortly before I moved to Scotland. It was now 1989. I spent a few days in London with my sister and my parents. It was my first time in the Capital and I can recall how busy and complicated it was, with all the traffic, the subway trains and the huge towering glass buildings. There's something compelling about the mix of architecture, too. The way that modern buildings litter the skyline, living alongside older buildings which first set the foundations for London as we know it.

During our visit, we went to Madame Tussaud's. The infamous wax works were amazing, their life like appearances and the opportunity to stand alongside celebrities can be too good to resist. This was before the time when people carried mobile phones with them and many tourists carried those big old spool cameras strapped around their neck.

I can't remember the detail of the entire visit, but I do recall the sense of fear as I encountered a mysterious black shadow amongst the exhibits (I also remember eating Chinese chicken wings in a park in Central London as we enjoyed a picnic. Isn't it funny how these memories come back to us later on?).

Mum and dad were standing with my sister, reading the names of sporting celebrities, mounted to the wax works on a little plaque. I was there, too, standing off to one side. It was really busy and tourists from all over the world moved around, laughing and joking as they took photographs. Everyone was enjoying themselves, having fun. I'm not sure what drew my attention first. Thinking back, it was the sense that something extraordinary was present. At this time in my life, I didn't know or understand the things that I was experiencing. I knew about ghosts, but I didn't *really* know. The hairs on the back of my neck began to stand on end and my skin began to twitch. It's a bit like a fly hitting a spider's web. I call it my 'spidey sense' like in the film *Spiderman*. It alerts me to activity in the same way that a spider knows that a fly is trapped in its web.

As we are walking around, I see something from the corner of my eye. A slight movement behind one of the wax works. I look carefully and see a shadow which doesn't belong there. I mean, it doesn't look right to me. It's odd, a funny mist that changes shape a few times within the space of seconds. It hovers a few feet above the floor and I instinctively know that it's watching me. I'm not sure why it takes an interest in me. I know it's a man and I think he's dressed in some sort of cloth that resembles a sack. I can't see him, but I know he is there and what he looks like. I don't understand how I know this. And then he rushes at me. I'm taken by surprise at the sudden surge of energy and I know it's a ghost. Or rather my understanding of what a ghost looks like from the TV. I step back and my arm instinctively covers my face. As it nears me, the apparition evaporates and disappears before it gets close and I know that I've just experienced something supernatural.

I'm left in shock and somewhat afraid. I turn to

other people around me to see that no one else has witnessed this event. Unaware of the paranormal activity around them, they're still laughing at a joke that I'm not party to. My family are moving away now and I follow them towards the next exhibit. I don't look back, worried that whoever it was is still behind me.

And so, following this incident I then tried my best to avoid these kinds of encounters. I still visited castles and towers and old buildings, but I sort of 'switched' myself off. The closest I came again, was a visit to Stirling Castle a few years later. There are two areas within the Castle which invoked a similar response and I again knew that I was sensing spirit. My thinking had evolved somewhat at this stage and I knew the difference between a ghost and spirit. I've never been back to the castle to investigate my previous experiences, although I did have my wedding photos taken there in 2004. For your benefit, I can tell you that there is something in the Argyll museum. It's not sinister but it *is* spirit and it takes an interest in those visiting the exhibition. The second is a little scarier. A not-so-nice presence in the very bottom of a stairwell near the kitchen. I can't recall the name of the area, other than the fact that you descend a number of steps into what I can best describe as a dungeon. A feeling of being trapped and a man who can at best be described as nasty, cowering in the corner of the room, waiting to lash out at anyone who comes near to him.

A nasty spirit lurks beneath Stirling Castle, waiting to lash out at anyone who ventures near.

Photograph with my sister and dog, taken on the day that I saw a young boy in spirit. Tillicoultry, Scotland (1992).

When I was thirteen, I was out walking with my mum and sister and our dog, Cindy. She was a small white terrier cross. She was my second dog, my first being an amazing border collie named, Roy. He was loyal to me and he was very protective. On this sunny day, we were walking along a path known as the Devonway. It connects Tillicoultry to Dollar in Central Scotland. There is an old metal bridge at the back of Sterling Mills. It's all gated off now and is unsafe, but at the time it was completely open and you could walk across it. Cindy liked to dip her feet in the river that ran beneath the bridge. Crossing to the other side, my sister and I were messing around and from the corner of my eye, I saw a boy around 10 years of age. He had black hair and was dressed in blue clothes. He stared back at us from the tree line. Startled, I turned to face him, not realising that he wasn't actually there. As I did so, he disappeared in front of me! I alerted my mum and my sister and we had a look around the area, but there was no boy to be found. Interestingly, although I've never researched the area, there are ruins of an old building amongst the trees and I have the impression that this was related to coal mining. I suspect that the boy had passed away in the area due to an accident.

I'm often asked questions about spirit and my interactions with them. I can count on two hands the number of times that I have seen spirit and interacted with them in the exact same way that I would interact with you. This is called a reciprocal apparition. I guess that's more times than most people, but I certainly don't go around speaking to the dead as if I was the boy from the movie *Sixth Sense*, working with a deceased Bruce Willis (ok, so I admit that I didn't see that one coming but I can be a bit slow at times). I cannot speak for other mediums, but the media, TV and film have vastly overplayed these interactions. My physical encounters with ghostly apparitions and spirit tend to be brief. Today, much of what I perceive is happening in my mind's eye. It's hard to explain, but I will do so later when I talk about developing your own awareness of spirit. The most perplexing case that I wish to tell you about, was my visit to Cowane's Hospital in Stirling.

Cowane's Hospital is an interesting place. It's located in what I'd call the historical part of Stirling, nestled between the Church of the Holyrood, the cemetery and the Old Town Jail. I know the building well, as I once rented the studio, a small room in the

North Wing. I really loved my room, with its wood burning stove and the wooden floor boards. I used it for spiritual development workshops, teaching and for private sittings. I had a few unsettling experiences there. I once took my kids to visit and they hated it, but couldn't quite understand why. Before I took up my residency, I had arranged to meet a member of staff for a tour. I had arrived earlier than expected and so I took it upon myself to have a look around, and to get a feel for the place. I was walking around the grounds when I met a man named William. I can't remember any details about him other than that he had a pony tail. He told me that he was a caretaker and he would be happy to show me around. I spent around twenty minutes with him that day. We laughed and joked and he pointed out some of the building features. When the time came for my appointment, I thanked him for his time and then reported to the office. I met the member of staff with whom I had a prearranged meeting. She'd retrieved the key to the studio and when she offered me a tour, I declined and explained that William had shown me around. I was both shocked and amazed at her reply. There was no one named William working in the building. I described him and she did not recognise him. What gave me a real sense of the chills, was when I later mentioned this to the onsite café proprietor and he told me that their CCTV had once captured an apparition. He dug out the photograph from a desk drawer and shown it to me. It was the same man! Upon further investigation, I managed to find records of previous employees, to discover that a man named William (known as Bill) had been employed in 1974. Could this have been my wayward guide from the past?

END OF CHAPTER REFLECTION

Have you ever experienced something paranormal or anything spiritual? Have you had your own spooky encounters? If you have, think about what happened. What were you doing at the time and who were you with?

I recommend that you keep a diary for a two week period. Try to take notice of any synchronicities, coincidences or connections that you experience. Spirit work in patterns and they'll communicate with you all the time. Slowing down your life and taking note of the things around you is the first step in raising your spiritual awareness. Begin to talk to them (you can do this in your head!) and ask for a reply. Don't worry if you don't see or hear their response. Mediumship takes time and patience and it isn't something that you can switch on or off over night. Forget what you *think* you know and just let it happen naturally.

GROWING UP

"Spirit can inhabit new places too, either because they're built upon something older, or because something old has been introduced to the building, for example, an old chair, doll or item that has an attached spirit."

As I moved into my teenage years, I tried to tell my friends and family that I could experience interactions with spirit. I used to do this crazy thing, and would say '*lifeline*' whenever I had a connection. I've no idea why, but it must have made sense to me at the time. Of course, my friends thought I was completely crazy and I was often on the receiving end of their jokes. Despite this, the things that I could see, feel and hear would not go away. Over time, I learned to deal with it as things came and went.

I was nearing the completion of my studies at university, where I was training to become a teacher. Even then, I felt the need to help others understand the world around them. But the constant bombardment of information and uncertainty on how I was to react to these interactions led me to alcohol. Don't get me wrong, I was never in a position where

I made myself vulnerable or where I regularly hit the bottom of a bottle, but I did spend an extraordinary amount of cash. I remember using a good proportion of my student grant on Vodka, and at the time, as I was working with a large supermarket chain as a back shift supervisor, I had a mediocre income.

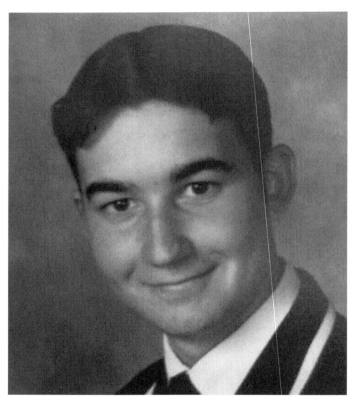

My final year at school, aged 17 (1997).

At the height of my drinking, I would appear at the bar in the local pool hall and the lady behind the counter would simply hand over two glasses containing a mixture of vodka and cola. I didn't need to ask for it as she already knew what I would order, and it always came in two glasses against everyone else's one glass. If nothing else, I was a creature of habit. The alcohol worked to an extent. It allowed me to forget about the spirit world and it provided me with an escape. But it was *always* a temporary escape from reality and it came at a cost... both in monetary value and in my own sanity.   And then at the turn of the Century, in the year 2000, something strange happened. An experience that I'll never forget.

I'd been at the pool hall with one of my friends, Pete. It was the middle of the afternoon and the hall was quiet. I was driving that day and hadn't been drinking, and we started to chat to the bar hostess, Liz. She told us that she was a student at the University of Stirling, and that she was studying a degree in psychology, with a special interest in parapsychology. She was conducting experiments into symbiotic relationships between human subjects and she wanted two 'guinea pigs' for her experiment as part of her final dissertation.

Now, you need to understand that Pete and I were good friends, we'd worked with each other for a few years at the supermarket and we were always game for a laugh. So we agreed to take part. My memory of the event is clear, which is a surprise given that I have a memory like a sieve and that this was around twenty years ago.

It was dark outside, though it was early in the evening, perhaps 6pm or thereabouts. It was late in November and the Christmas tunes had started to appear on the radio. Pete and I met outside the faculty building on the university campus, and then wandered through the labyrinth of corridors and passages until we found the room in the basement. It was actually a large room, but was divided into smaller areas and (from what I recall) little sound proofed rooms like what a recording artist would use.

Liz was waiting for us and as we signed the paperwork, she explained to us what would happen as participants in the experiment. Pete and I were placed into different rooms. They were dark, and we could not see or hear anything. I had electrodes strapped to my head via what looked like a shower cap, as did Pete. We had been laughing at each other as we put on the kit, which probably took much longer than it needed to as we were fooling around, much to the annoyance of Liz. As I sat in the sensory deprivation room, I simply had to think about Pete. And that's exactly what I did. I was in that booth for around half an hour. What I didn't know at the time, was that in his room, he was listening to an assortment of music. Various genres were playing from rock to classical. As he listened, a sophisticated computer programme was mapping his brainwave patterns onto a sheet of paper, outside in the main lab area. That same programme was also mapping my brainwave patterns.

Afterwards, we were asked to sit down and it was explained to us that the purpose of the experiment was to seek evidence that two people could synchronise their brainwave patterns without being in the same room. I remember to this day, the lock of amazement in Liz's eyes as she held onto the papers, her hand shaking slightly as she explained that there was a clear correlation between my patterns and Pete's. Simply by thinking about him, I was somehow able to tune into what he was thinking and feeling and my mind began to imitate his thoughts patterns. She spoke to us about empathy and about these connections that she was exploring and it occurred to me that what she was describing was like a form of human WiFi. As we left her that night, she laughed on our way out and shouted after me.

"Lee, you must be psychic."

I laughed and returned an 'okay' sign to her. After this, I rarely drank again. Something profound had happened and it shifted my mindset.

I graduated in 2001 from the University of Strathclyde and used my teaching degree to work in a number of schools around Scotland. During my career, I often experienced things as I had done when I was younger, but I simply ignored it. I was focussed on work and this had become my new escape.

I hadn't been teaching for long when I began to notice something wasn't right physically. I've actually had remarkable health and never really experienced many childhood ailments. The only thing I'd ever had, beside the usual colds, was tonsillitis. I'd escaped all the other bugs that went around family and friends. I remember when I was around seven or eight years old, a chicken pox epidemic floored every single person in my class at school. I was exposed, as I spent time with friends in the street where I lived, yet I never did contract the virus. I thought that I was indestructible.

So when I started to become tired, unwell and when I suffered pains in my abdomen, feet and legs, I knew something was up. I made an appointment at the local general practitioner and a diagnosis came shortly, thereafter. I was told, as the doctor studied my notes, that I'd had a pneumococcal infection in my upper respiratory system. True, I remember this, as I'd had a few weeks off work and university with what I thought has been a bad cold. I was given antibiotics at the time. I listened intently as the doctor told me that medical research had linked respiratory conditions as a contributing factor in the development of a condition called Henoch-Schönlein Purpura (HSP), which is a systemic vasculitis which can affect the skin, joints, bowel and kidneys. It is also known as IgA vasculitis (IgAV). IgA is a form of antibody that we all make, to protect the lining of the airway, throat, and gut. If IgA gets stuck in the smaller blood vessels it causes inflammation (vasculitis) and this is termed IgAV. Sometimes IgA will get stuck in the small vessels in the kidney and is called Henoch-Schönlein Nephritis or Vasculitic IgA Nephropathy. Essentially, this is something that I've lived with since I was around 20 years old. It's manageable and doesn't really cause many problems, though every now and again I do become really tired as a result. I also need to limit my coffee intake (which I am very bad at) and also my alcohol intake (which I am very good at – I have not had a drink for 15 years). These are triggers for my HSP.

I married Claire in 2004 and we had a son in 2006 and a daughter in 2008. My career in education was at new heights. I'd already been promoted to Principal Teacher in a secondary school and I had enjoyed a secondment to the Scottish Government. I was much older by this time and in 2012, I began working at the University of Glasgow as a Senior Lecturer. It was through my academic work when I travelled abroad, and took the opportunity to investigate spirit further afield.

I had started to feel a pull, like a deep need to satisfy something within myself, and I was fortunate to spend time in Romania, Bulgaria and Australia. The City of Sofia is an amazing place and is built upon the remains of one of the oldest Cities in the world. If you've never been, I strongly recommend a visit. I was to discover upon my arrival, that the hotel in which I was staying was built up on an old Roman amphitheater. When the building was being excavated, they dug beneath the foundations to build the planned spa and swimming pool, only to discover the ruins. That put a stop to those plans. One evening, I was waiting for colleagues in the lobby (we did that often) and from the corner of my eye, I saw a Roman

Centurion glide across the floor. I say glide, as I couldn't actually see his legs. He 'terminated' just below the waste. I asked the receptionist to tell me about the ruins, and I was surprised to hear that the original floor had been preserved. The tiles upon which I stood were now suspended about three foot above the original. Could this have explained the reason why I saw him from waste upwards? Not all old buildings are haunted. The hotel was reasonably modern, and I also encountered the spirit of a lady in a nearby restaurant. Spirit can inhabit new places too, either because they're built upon something older, or because something old has been introduced to the building, for example, an old chair, doll or item that has an attached spirit.

It was in the summer of 2013 when something happened that would change my life forever. I had been working in my private office at the university. I was sat at my desk when I became aware of a presence next to me. As I turned, I nearly fell off my chair as I saw a young man standing only a few feet away. He was around my height, with short black hair and a dark complexion. He stared at me, but didn't speak. In that moment, I somehow knew that his name was Mark, that he was 21 years old and that he had been killed on a motorcycle. The encounter lasted less than a minute and then he was gone. What really struck me, a few weeks prior, I had been party to a medium who had visited the house. I've had a few readings in my time, and nearly all those reading me had told me that I had the ability to do what they do. One of these mediums, who would later become a teacher to me, had told me that if I ever needed to learn more about mediumship, I should contact her. So I thought about this for a week or two and during that time, Mark would appear to me twice more.

I spent eight weeks shadowing my new teacher, as she took me through her workshops and lessons, to help me make sense of the things that I has been experiencing all my life. Three months after Mark had first appeared in my office, I told Claire that I was ready to start reading people. She arranged for three people (she knew them but I didn't) to come to our house. I had purchased my first set of tarot cards from a book store and had been swatting up on their meaning. As I started to read those three woman, Mark appeared again. I was sat in my kitchen at the time, reading these ladies one at a time. I described him to each of them, only for them to tell me that they didn't understand that connection.

I'm crap at this, I thought to myself. I pushed on, and gave them other connections and messages that made more sense. And then something magical happened. Two weeks later, one of the ladies reached out to me. She had told her husband about the reading and his face had drained white. Shaking, he told his wife that when he was a teenager, one of his friends had died, having driven into the back of a truck on his motorbike. He was 21 years old at the time and his name was Mark.

This was a valuable lesson to me. Many of us expect that during a reading, we will encounter our own loved ones and direct family members. This is often the case, but there have been many instances where I have facilitated readings and an old neighbor from twenty years ago, or a childhood friend has come through. It also served as a confirmation to me, that I was doing the right thing. I had always been spiritually aware, but now I was learning to use it to help other people. A burning desire was building within me, to teach others about life and to help them understand what it meant to be alive.

To me, the meaning of life is to learn, so that our soul can progress onto the next life that we'll experience. We all have lessons and some may be aware of what those lessons are, but for most of us, we'll meander through life and only when we die, will we then reflect and understand what we've just experienced in our physical form.

It was all falling into place. I would think about what was going on within and around me as I would fall asleep at night. In late December 2013, I fell asleep after such a pondering and I met someone in my dream. He told me that his name was Harold, and that he would be my guide.

On location in the Roman ruins in Sofia, Bulgaria (2013).

On location in the church crypts, Romania (2014).

On location in a painted church, Romania (2014).

END OF CHAPTER REFLECTION

Consider these typical signs of spiritual awakening. Have you experienced any of them? Tick the signs that resonate with you.

- ✓ Increased empathy and the feeling that you're connected to the people around you.
- ✓ Feeling adverse to negative people or behaviours.
- ✓ You find it hard to worry about things and become less concerned with material life.
- ✓ You find yourself drawn to nature.
- ✓ You become sensitive to light.
- ✓ You feel an overwhelming need to help people.
- ✓ You desire a sense of belonging and community.
- ✓ You feel as though you've found inner peace.
- ✓ You experience regular spirit interactions.
- ✓ You have vivid dreams and find that you're easily distracted.
- ✓ You begin to understand your life purpose and you're excited about new experiences.

SPIRIT GUIDES

"You will have at least one guide. If you don't know who they are, my advice is to simply ask them to make themselves known to you."

We all have spirit guides. There are many guides around us who come to us for different reasons. They could be Master Guides or Gatekeepers, or they could be guides with specific purpose such as helping us with matters of relationships, health or finances. Depending who you ask, you'll get different opinions on guides, who they are, and why they are present at any particular time. Most people go through life without any conscious connection to their guides. Their journey continues as they are blissfully unaware that a greater power is helping them along the way.

The first guide that I became aware of was named Joe. He's a ten year old boy who appears to me now and again. When I see him, I know that he's there to remind me to have fun, as my life can become quite serious at times and I admit that there have been occasions when I tend to work too much, to the detriment of family time and relaxation. I first met Joe during a meditation. I was in an old rowing boat on the ocean. Joe would tell me jokes and he would tell me to relax and let things happen naturally. He helped me to understand that working with spirit and using mediumship is not something that can be forced. Many people make that mistake, for example, when they're on a paranormal investigation, in trying really hard to 'see' or 'hear' spirit. In fact, they are more likely to experience something if they relax their mind and allow things to just happen around them.

Remember my experience with the old man in the abandoned building. He appeared to me when I wasn't expecting him. This is often how things work out. It's got very little to do with spirit, but more to do with your own mindset. I'll talk to you more about that later on in the chapter that I've called *Intuitive Perception*.

After I met Joe, Harold then came to me in my sleep. He introduced himself by name. I was sat upon a stone wall along a cliff edge, overlooking the ocean. At the time, I knew very little about him but I somehow knew that I was in Ancient Greece. The architecture of the buildings around me and the clothing that people wore gave it away. Anyone who knows me as a medium will be able to tell you that I'm rubbish when it comes to clothing and identifying the year. I can be on location and I could see spirit wearing some sort of garment and although I could describe it, I'm clueless to the time period. With Harold, I'd seen enough movies and TV shows to recognise this period in history, even if I didn't know the exact year.

I was attending a spiritual development circle which was hosted by a friend who was also a medium. I hadn't told anyone about my encounter with my new guide, so imagine my surprise when my medium friend told me that she was sensing the name 'Harold' around me! This was amazing validation to me. More was yet to come as details began to reveal themselves. This happened over several weeks early in 2015. In April, I had asked someone (whom I'd found online) to draw a spirit guide portrait for me. I'd found her website by chance after a friend of mine had mentioned her to me in passing. Nelly Moon is a psychic artist and a medium and she works to connect people to their guides. She is probably the most knowledgeable person that I know when it comes to spirit guides.

I had never met her before and she knew nothing about me, other than my name and a photograph that I had sent to her. At this time, I didn't have any social media presence or a website and so there was no way that she could have known anything about me. I'd kept my contact with her a secret. A few days after I had emailed her, she sent me a picture of my guide along with some information about him. My heart was racing as I read what she had sent to me. I know it sounds daft, but I actually felt quite tearful. A profound sense of completion hit me and it felt like the foundations had been laid, on which I could finally continue my spiritual journey, begin to know myself and rest assured that someone 'had my back'.

In writing this book, I decided to share with you

the email exchange and the words that were sent between myself and Nelly. I have her permission to share these details with you, as they are personal to us.

"Dear Lee... After meditating on your image I am now convinced the guide that has visited me several times in my dreams is connected to you. The name he gives is Atticus and he is an ancient although I'm unsure if he is from Rome or Greece. I'm also convinced he is your gatekeeper as he is giving very little information. I have no idea why gatekeepers tend to be quiet, maybe it's because they are with you to offer protection and part of them is also protecting themselves. Atticus is showing me parallel lines so I feel either there is a past life connection with him, or during his life on earth there are connections with the work he did to what you have done or are now doing. He comes through holding a spear (which is another reason I think he is your gatekeeper) but also a scroll. From that I feel within your work or life you deal with words, either teaching or recording facts

or information. Atticus was a man of words, a teacher and philosopher and he also mentions his love of architecture and politics and his love of debates. I should imagine he was very well educated and rose to a high level of importance during the time he was walking the earth. He shows himself to me as an elderly man dressed in robes. Atticus is your gatekeeper, your guide of Protection and he comes through holding a spear and scroll."

Courtesy of Nelly Moon, this image illustrates my spirit guide and gatekeeper, Harold.

I was shocked. If you've read thus far you will realise that Harold and I have much in common. Our parallel lines and interests in teaching, politics and architecture is too much to be coincidental. I sent back in response to this message.

"Dear Nelly… I have been aware of a connection to spirit all my life and only recently have I started to make direct use of it. I have also felt on a 'path' regarding my career and things have fallen into place for me since I can remember. As if someone else is making things happen around me. My career has came about by being in the right place at the right time on a few occasions. I am indeed a teacher. In fact, I lecture at the University of Glasgow - I teach teachers. I also engage in scholarship and research. Not only that, but my interests in design and technology (my subject area) also includes architecture. In fact, only last week have I found myself pulled into a new building project at the university. A few years ago I worked for a short period with the Scottish Government. So teaching,

scholarship, writing, architecture and politics is essentially who I am. Sound familiar!? I have been aware for some time of a guide around me who for some reason I call Harold (the name came to me in my sleep). It could be a coincidence but when you told me the name Atticus I instantly thought Haroldus Atticus lol. I decided to Google him. I found an Ancient Greek named Herodes Atticus (and a range of other Middle names they tended to do that in those days) who fits the bill exactly. I am strongly drawn to this man and get the strangest feeling when I read about him. His bust portrait doesn't look miles away from your portrait either. If you google Herodes Atticus you'll see what I mean. This is also timely as I am struggling to balance spirit, work at the university and family right now and feel that I am about to change the way that I work. Atticus is indeed very protective and he tends to step in when my workload increases like this. It's happened twice before. Other mediums have sensed him too on a few occasions and once a medium performing reiki actually told me that a man in robes was pushing her away from me trying to protect me! Anyway, regardless of the connection, thanks so much for the portrait and the information. Whether it is Herodes Atticus or just Atticus does not matter to me. The fact he's there is what gives comfort."

You'll see in my reply, that I referred to some research that I had undertaken. Many guides are not written in history, but I feel lucky that I have been able to piece together many sources of information to identify mine. I call him Harold, though his real name is Atticus Herodes (or Herodes Atticus). He is an ancient Greek aristocrat and sophist who lived between AD 101-177. We also knew each other when fighting at Thermopylae as Spartans, and as priests in the Court of Alfred the Great.

He has appeared in many forms over the years but I have only recently recognised this. Harold appeared to Nelly holding a spear (my protection) and a scroll (for we share a passion for scholarship, teaching, politics and architecture). Appointed consul at Rome in 143, he was the first Greek to hold the rank of consul ordinarius, as opposed to consul suffectus. In Latin, his full name was given as Lucius Vibullius Hipparchus Tiberius Claudius Atticus Herodes. According to Philostratus, he was a notable proponent of the Second Sophistic. Herodes Atticus was born in Marathon, Greece and spent his childhood years between Greece and Italy. According to Juvenal Satire III, he received an education in rhetoric and philosophy from many of the best teachers from both Greek and Roman culture. Throughout his life, however, Herodes Atticus remained entirely Greek in his cultural outlook. The Roman Emperor Hadrian in 125 appointed him Prefect of the free cities in the Roman province of Asia. He later returned to Athens, where he became famous as a teacher. In the year 140, Herodes Atticus was elected and served as an Archon of Athens. Later, the Roman Emperor Antoninus Pius invited him to Rome from Athens to educate his two adopted sons, who were the future Roman Emperors Marcus Aurelius and Lucius Verus. Sometime after Herodes Atticus came to Rome from

Athens he was betrothed to Aspasia Annia Regilla, a wealthy aristocrat, who was related to the wife of Antoninus Pius, Empress Faustina the Elder. As Herodes Atticus was in favor with the Emperor, as a mark of his friendship Antoninus Pius appointed him Consul in 143.

Interestingly, the name Herodes has all but vanished over the years and in modern times many have translated it into Harold! So, you'll see that I'm fortunate to know my guide. I have a strong connection to him and he is always there for me. I have had other guides come and go over the years, but he has remained constant.

I was once investigating alleged paranormal activity at a World War II aircraft hanger in Grangemouth, Scotland. During the investigation, the team and I were sat around a table with a Ghostbox. This was one of the early devices that scanned radio frequencies and spat out static white noise. Every now and again, it would pick up a word or phrase. The idea was that we would ask out loud, questions to spirit and they would then seek to try and talk to us. I asked for spirit to name someone sat at the table and as witnessed by several people, the device proceeded to speak all our names in turn. We were astonished, especially when the last word was spoken. *Harold.* Sadly, we had not expected such validation and we had not recorded this.

You will have at least one guide. If you don't know who they are, my advice is to simply ask them to make themselves known to you. You can do this during mediation, or in that time where you're in bed and about to fall asleep, asking them to come to you in your dream state. But remember that you can't force this and they will only let themselves be known to you if they feel this is needed and that you're ready. I know many mediums who work with spirit but they are not aware of their guides.

You can also try a guided meditation. There are many free ones available on *YouTube*. You may need to try a few before you find one that works for you. Take your time with this. Guides do not appear as most spirit do. That is, I have only ever seen Harold once in shadow form.

Guides do not 'talk' to us either. I don't hear Harold's voice as I hear you speak to me. Instead, he whispers to my soul and shows me things. This form of intuitive perception comes naturally to me, but it is something that we can all learn. You need to train your mind to enter a different 'mode' that allows you to push your logic brain to one side and accept the signs, symbols and messages that spirit places in front of you. I'm often asked if I can 'shut off' from spirit and in short, the answer is no. This is perfectly normal for me and it's just an accepted part of my life and who I am. I'm not particularly religious but spirituality is a faith of sorts. My faith and my religion is what I make for myself. I do not believe in a God (or multiple gods for that matter) but I do believe that there is a greater power or a source of energy from which we all originate.

Likewise, I do not believe in heaven or hell, but I do believe that there is another state of existence where spirit resides. This is not a physical place and time and physics as we understand it does not apply in the same way as it does to us here on this Earth plane. This is why we have difficulty trying to explain what 'heaven' looks like.

That all said, protection is essential when working with spirit. I always protect myself and others regardless of the type of work in which I'm about to engage. Protection is all about your mindset. There are many people who use crystals and runes to protect themselves and that's fine. I've done the same on occasion. The most important thing is to visualise the protection and to believe in it. This is where our guides are important. They keep us safe and later on, I'll give you some examples of how Harold has kept me safe from harm. Yes, I did 'sick up a spirit', but I'll talk about that when I discuss paranormal investigation with you.

So how do I protect myself?

I open up with a short prayer. The words are not particularly important, but the sentiment and meaning is crucial. I visualise in my mind, a white bubble of protection around my body. If you like, it's my aura, pushed out and surrounded by the light and protection of the universe.

"I ask the Higher Side of Life for Protection. I ask my guides to come forward and to help me communicate with spirit. I ask spirit to come forward and to pass on messages. To let themselves be known, to be seen and to be heard. I now leave myself open to spirit under the protection of my guides, Amen."

I always extend this protection to anyone with me during a paranormal investigation or when I'm attending someone else's home for a private sitting or group reading. They don't necessarily know that I've done this, but it makes me feel better knowing that I have done so. Afterwards, I say similar words and thank my guides for their protection. This closing down is important. I still experience things, but to a lesser extent as Harold knows that I'm not actively seeking to work with them.

I once came home from a reading and it was late at night. I went to bed without closing down and I was awakened in the middle of the night. I'd had a nightmare about a young teenage girl with cancer. Her face was as white as a sheet and she had no hair.

Sweating, I then realised that Claire was awake beside me. She told me she'd had a bad dream about someone wearing a white mask. Again, I don't believe in coincidences and we had shared a connection with spirit that night. Mediums act as a magnet to spirit and we'd been visited by this young lady, whom I was later able to connect to someone during a reading. It's quite common for me to find that spirit drop in ahead of a reading. Sometimes, this happens weeks before I even know that I'm about to meet someone, as it did with Mark that day in my office at the university.

END OF CHAPTER REFLECTION

There are many guided meditations available on *YouTube*. Some are better than others and you may need to try a few until you find one that works for you. When you meditate, don't worry about breathing in and out in a certain way, or trying to 'clear your mind'. Instead, just relax and imagine yourself sinking into your seat. Breath and sit in a way that's comfortable to you. Become aware of all the aches and pains in your body and imagine the muscles beginning to unwind. The tension gradually leaving your body.

Try to imagine yourself walking through a green forest. In a clearing ahead, your guide is waiting for you at a bench. Try to visualise a conversation with them in your head. A guided meditation will help you with this visualisation. Who are they? Do they give you a name? Each time that you do this, take a note on anything that you experience. Don't worry about forcing things and if you don't get anything or you just see colours, that's not unusual.

ETERNAL SOUL

"When our soul comes across someone else on the same spiritual plane, we feel connected, even for a few moments in time and there's often a mutual understanding between the two."

We've lived many lives before. Our soul is eternal and our single purpose in life, what some would call the meaning of life, is to learn and to advance to a higher spiritual plane of existence. I guess you could also refer to this as enlightenment or ascension.

We meet different people along the way. You may have experienced a time when you met someone for the first time and you instantly liked them. You may even have a strong feeling that you've met them before. This is because you've encountered their soul in another lifetime. Your conscious mind cannot understand the memories buried deep within your psyche. The opposite is also true. You may meet someone and find that you instantly dislike them, but you don't understand where this feeling comes from. Perhaps they've harmed you in the past, or they've done something to cause this emotional reaction.

I also have another theory about these first encounters with other souls. Some believe that there are several 'planes of existence' on the Higher Side of Life and that we advance through these as we mature in spirit. Our understanding of the universe becomes broader, deeper and can be applied to science as well as to the paranormal. They're not as separated as some may want to believe. When our soul comes across someone else on the same spiritual plane, we feel connected, even for a few moments in time and there's often a mutual understanding between the two. This can be profound when the connection is also made to someone known to us from another lifetime. Many people talk about meeting their 'soulmate' and this is exactly the situation that I'm describing.

So, how does all this past life and reincarnation stuff work? To answer that, I'll give you some examples of my own. I've managed to piece together aspects of my past lives. Or at least a few of them. There are some that I want to share with you. I've been fortunate to have experienced regression and through a deep state of relaxation, in a trance like state, I've described to others a battle in which I fought with the Knights Templar in the ancient city of Acre, circa 1200AD. I was killed protecting people from an attacking enemy and was shot with an arrow which took several days to finally end me. My lesson in this time was one of sacrifice and circumstance, being in the right place at the right time and doing the right thing. These connections have existed in other experiences that I've had.

Living as a young woman in the ancient Ottoman Empire where my entire village was poisoned by an enemy, fighting at the battle of Thermopylae (with Harold!) in 480 BC and a strong affinity to Alfred the Great as a priest attending his court. It was during this latter lifetime where I developed my love for learning and education.

Perhaps the strongest past life experience that I have ever experienced came from reoccurring dreams that I have on a regular basis. In this dream, I'm around 23 years of age. I left my wife and my children to fight in the Second World War. I recall saying goodbye to them, the detail of the cottage where I lived clear as day. I hugged them individually, promising them that I would return. I handed my son a small toy truck as a parting gift.

I never did return.

I fought in several battles around France. I passed to the Higher Side of Life having walked through a field, a single shot struck me in the upper right hand side of my back, near my shoulder and I recall falling face first into the mud as the impact took me off my feet. I could smell the dirt as it stuck to me. Again, as it once was in Thermopylae and in Acre, I had sacrificed myself in war, however here the lesson was one of equilibrium. To find a balance between duty and family.

I failed to learn that lesson all those years ago. Instead, I've had to learn it now in this life. I have a successful career and I've advanced to a job role which is prominent in my field of study. I'm well paid, yet I'm rarely satisfied as the balance of work, play and family is still not correct.

Having recalled details of the life I had before, I've been able to make the changes needed to learn. I still have work to do, but for now my soul feels at peace. Our lifetime can reveal many lessons to us and I'll need to remain vigilant to understand what they are. Accepting our strengths and our own weaknesses is the first step in correcting the actions and behaviours that have gone before.

I'm a great believer that we control our destiny. Spirit will guide us along the way and they may tell us the outcome of future events, but the journey is ours to make. We control our own actions and behaviours.

I often talk about an 'anchor' when I speak to people. This is a moment in time when something happens for a reason. A crossroads or a situation which forces us to choose a certain pathway or a fork in the road ahead. My advice to anyone uncertain is two-fold. First, consider doing nothing as sometimes, the right course of action reveals itself in time. Second, always follow your instinct. This is easier said than done as we tend to allow our logic brain to take over. It's not often that the two are aligned, but when they are, we know right away what needs to be done.

History is rich with stories of people with a talent for art, music, maths, science and language. Or perhaps someone has a unique skill or ability to do something that no one else can. I know that these abilities often come from a past life. For example, someone who speaks several languages or lived in other countries in the past, may now have the ability for phonics in their current life.

The Greats of our time, those we'd call geniuses such as Mozart and Einstein, were able to tap into a hidden memory without even realising that it was happening. And sometimes, young children will recall these memories and describe things that have happened, such as how they have died previously. A fear of water, or heights, or enclosed spaces. These could be suppressed fears bought on by something traumatic in our past that we just can't quite put our finger on. Or perhaps an injury now is related to another life. I recently had to have surgery on my right shoulder in the same place where I was shot during the Second World War!

That was an interesting experience. I was put under a general anesthetic, my first and only time. I recall the surgeons administrating an injection and asking me to count backwards from 10 to 1. As I started, I became aware of a spirit man at the side of the bed, dressed in an old robe. He looked a bit like a monk and he was smiling at me. I had only counted to 7 and that's the last thing that I remember. My surgery was a success and as I came back, I was disorientated and a bit out of it. I grabbed at the oxygen mask strapped to my face and pulled it off. The nurse rushed over and told me to relax. She laughed as she helped me remove the mask and told me that they thought I was never going to come around. Oddly, she told me that I'd been making sounds as if I'd been talking to someone. Perhaps it was a result of the medication and painkillers, but I suspect something else had been happening.

This raises a common question. For those who have had surgery, or those who have had one foot in this world and one in the next (for example, they have died for 30 seconds before being resuscitated), they often can't recall anything. I don't remember any details of being under the anesthetic, but it appears that I was experiencing something. So if someone dies, and then comes back, but can't recall the glorious afterlife, does this mean that we have it all wrong?

I don't believe that to be the case. For a long time, I've pondered what happens to the soul when we die. I've read a lot of literature on the subject matter over the years and in working with spirit, I've made my conclusions on this. Don't get me wrong, I don't have all the answers and I certainly don't have a fixed mindset. My thinking on this will continue to evolve. My interpretation is that we are not permitted to remember these details, just as when we reincarnate, we are not allowed to remember the details of the previous life that we've had.

Sometimes, we read in the media that a child tells a parent that they've died by drowning or on some occasions, they've even been able to give detailed information about themselves that upon checking, turns out to have some truth to it. As I've already said, we go through life and our soul learns many lessons. When we die, the soul, which is the term that I apply to our spiritual energy, leaves the physical body and rejoins the source from which we originate. Some may refer to this as heaven, though this isn't a place as we would imagine it. Rather, it's another state of existence that thrives in parallel to our own. At this point, our soul enters a period of reflection. We think about the life that we've just had and we seek to make sense of it all. For some, this may be a fast process but for others it may take years. For the few, they may never learn or grow or they may make the same mistakes several times over. During reflection, they may revisit the people that were around them in the physical world. Or they may visit a location where something happened that is important to their reflection. This could be a happy memory or something traumatic such as a murder. This spirit interaction is what we observe during a paranormal investigation, or through a reading.

The people within our lifetime have been known to us before. We may live life as a man or as a woman, or we may identify as something else. Our relationships may change, so a brother in one life time may be a father or a friend in another. Our reflection is not something that we do alone. We may need to interact with other souls to fully understand our lesson in life. This may be the form of closure from someone still living, or it may be that our soul is united with another on the Higher Side of Life.

Only once we have completed this reflection, will we come back in physical form. This could be on this Earth or on another world. There have been many reports that people undergoing past life regression, hypnosis or even walking memories remember living on a world with two suns, a purple sky and crystal like plant life.

I learned long ago not to worry about this or to try and analyse it. Life is much simpler if we accept this and focus instead on who we are *now* and what we are *doing* now.

I once gave a young lady a reading. Let's call her

Sophie to protect her identity. She was around 25 years old. Her friend had set up the reading for me as she was really struggling with life. Other than her name and address, I knew nothing about her. During the reading, her mum had come through from spirit and I was able to pass on messages that made sense to her. I then told her something incredible. It was almost mind blowing.

"They show me a young boy," I said. "He's around 4 years old."

Nodding eagerly, she confirmed that she did indeed have a son.

"What's his name?" I asked.

"Callum."

"Well," I started to explain. "Your mum wants you to know that she watches over him. She's noticed his runny nose and you'll need to keep an eye on that."

Sophie laughed. "Yeh, his nose has been runny for the last day or two. I was going to take him to the doctor as he's had a problem with it before."

"Ah, I see," I replied. "Your mum tells me

something else. You've lost a child that passed away."

Sophie looked at me, her expression of laughter now gone and a deep sadness penetrated her face.

"I believe this child died once he was born," I continued.

"Yes, that's right."

I didn't feel the need to probe into the detail. So I didn't ask her what had happened.

"I need to tell you something, but you can take it with a pinch of salt if you like."

"Okay," she said. I could hear the uncertainty in her voice. I decided to pass on the message.

"Your son was lost back to the Higher Side of Life as his soul was not compatible with his body. There was something wrong with it. But you need to know that he's with you again. Your mum tells me that you lost this child before you conceived Callum. His soul returned to you when that happened. Callum is the son that you lost."

She stared at me. I wasn't sure if she was going to hug me and cry, or cry and smack me. I don't always trust myself with the words that I speak as I'm only human and I make mistakes like anyone else, but spirit often give me the right things to say at the right time, and usually to the right person. I'm learning to trust in that.

"I can't believe that you've just told me that," she said. "I had a reading with another medium a few months ago and he told me the exact same thing almost word for word."

I smiled and we had a discussion on what I had experienced over the years. She told me more about her son. The reading concluded and it turned into a chat around spirituality and teaching. I find that people come for readings for different purposes. Sometimes they want to connect with a loved one who has passed over. Sometimes they want some guidance as they feel lost. Sometimes it's reassurance that they seek, or perhaps they're just looking for some entertainment. It doesn't really matter what their rationale is. But the one thing that they all have in common is an underlying thirst to know more about spirit. I believe that this is because deep down, our soul recognises itself in the conversation and we are all seeking to understand the meaning of life. We need a purpose and we want to understand what that purpose is. I found mine in 2014 during my time in Romania, where I had time to reflect on my own spirituality. My visitations to the monasteries and painted churches in Romania were especially profound and shortly thereafter, I was fortunate to spend time with children in a Roma school, as they explored life from a perspective that was alien to me. This served as a reminder that although we are all human, our experiences and knowledge of the world can be very different.

Visiting a Roma school, Romania (2014).

END OF CHAPTER REFLECTION

An empathic ability means that you're more likely to be susceptible to negative experiences. Meaningful interaction with spirit requires emotional resilience and an ability to switch your mind into a different mode. Do you recognise these signs in yourself?

- ✓ You instantly feel 'connected' to some people
- ✓ You worry about what others think about you
- ✓ You have many highs and many lows
- ✓ You can 'sense' emotions
- ✓ You put other people's needs before your own
- ✓ You absorb emotions like a sponge
- ✓ You prefer deep conversations over small talk
- ✓ You treat your pets like humans
- ✓ You find that people open up to you in confidence

Practice mediation to clear your mind and make sure that you 'open' and 'close' to spirit.

INTUITIVE

PERCEPTION

"You'll have heard of the elusive sixth sense. Well, that's what I call intuitive perception."

Throughout this book, I'm providing you with my insights and experiences, which lead me to make conclusions about spirit, mediumship and about life. But you can take as much or as little as you like. Over time, perceptions change. We learn lessons in life, we gain knowledge and we begin to think about life in a way that's not possible when we were children.

At the time of writing this book, I've been aware of spirit for 40 years and in that time, I've come to realise that life is like a fine tapestry. On the surface most see the beautiful image through design, but that design also covers something else. On the reverse, or underneath the image, are the stitches and threads that bind everything together, a bit like the mysterious sounds of the universe, the stars twinkling in time to an unheard tune. It resonates, but we're often too busy to stop and listen. We don't hear the music until the day that we become eternal and our energy once again rejoins the source from which we originate.

For now, we will need to be content with the beat, which drives our lives and creates a necessary interpretation of what goes on around us. You ARE the centre of the universe; so don't let anyone tell you otherwise. Of course, I refer to *your* universe and not *the* universe, but the line between the two is often blurred.

The theory of general relativity describes the universe under a system of field equations that determine the metric, or distance function of spacetime. There exist exact solutions to these equations; some point in the causal future of time is also in its causal past. Quantum-mechanical phenomena was referred to as *"spooky action at a distance"* by Einstein. A variation of Everett's many-worlds interpretation of quantum mechanics provides a resolution to the paradox that involves us arriving in a different dimension to the one we came from.

From a spiritual perspective, these theories are aligned to my own thoughts on how spirit interacts with us and I make two further conclusions. First, that time is not liner for spirit as it is for us. I mentioned earlier that it can take many years for a soul to complete a reflection on the life it's just had. That passage of time, whether it be 5 years, 50 years or even 500 years, is not a concept that is measured as we would consider it. The passage of time is not relative.

I've encountered many spirits whom have grown through the years, for example, where they've died as a child and then matured into adulthood. On other occasions, they've remained at the age they passed, or rarely, they've appeared to me younger than they were when they left their corporeal form. I clearly recall reading a lovely lady named Margaret from Stirling. Her grandfather come to her and I could see him standing in her lounge. Oddly, he looked to be black and white, like an image from an old TV set. When I described him, Margaret then produced the only photograph she had of her grandfather. I was shocked to see that it was black and white and it had been taken several years before he'd died. It was exactly as I'd seen him!

My second theory is related to the concept that ghosts and spirit are actually formed from the many-worlds paradox, and that we are inter dimensional beings jumping from one world to the next. The multi-verse (as it is often known), is a way of explaining probability and hypothetical statements regarding the shift between realities. Some philosophers such as David Lewis, believe that all possible worlds exist and that they are just as real as the world we live in.

Prior to the 20th century, it was a commonly held belief that nature itself was simple and that simpler hypotheses about nature were thus more likely to be true. This notion was deeply rooted in the aesthetic value that simplicity holds for human thought and the justifications presented for it often drew from theology. Thomas Aquinas made this argument in the 13th century, writing, *"If a thing can be done adequately by means of one, it is superfluous to do it by means of several; for we observe that nature does not employ two instruments if one suffices."*

My interpretation is thus; I believe that human beings are energy based life forms. The soul forms this energy and we have lived many lives before. I believe that some of those lives may have been spent on different worlds, but that those worlds are not inter-dimensional. Occam's razor is used as an heuristic in the development of theoretical models. In other words, the simplest explanation is often the correct one. Of course, this isn't scientific evidence and there are many sceptics who dispute this claim, though the scenario I've described thus far also marries with my own epistemological beliefs.

Beginning in the 20th century, epistemological justifications based on induction, logic, pragmatism, and especially probability theory have become more popular among philosophers.

I'm not going to get too deep here, but essentially you will need to be open minded and consider that time is not linear and that spirit is not bound to this Earth as we are in physical form. Psychics is a concept that is defined by our understanding and experience; in our own mind we can jump from the present to the past, our memories and thoughts resurfacing at recall. Occasionally, when external stimuli prompt something to surface; a smell, sound or an experiential event, we remember something that we hadn't thought about for a long time. It's incredible isn't it? We also have the ability to jump to future scenarios within our own mind. What if I was to tell you that you also live in the future. That's right, you can predict your own future – to an extent.

In my professional work, I consider myself to be a technologist and a futurist. Essentially, this is someone who considers the present (what we have already achieved), what is likely (following trends and global events) and exploring what is possible (or not possible) in the future. I like to think that my success is built upon the ability to see the bigger picture. Using my intuitive perception, I follow the guidance of universal energy and make a prediction on what is to come. You can try it, too.

It's never quite as easy as that, though. We can all make educated guesses, but to add in the detail, we need to explore something else entirely. This is where the power of your mind comes into play. It is my belief that a connection to a spiritual world is needed, where energy exists as a matter of course. It's all around us, a tapestry of colour and wonder. Some of us see and hear it more easily than others, but we can all tap into its potential. A mentalist would argue that the mind could be trained to think in a certain way. They are correct, but I would argue that a mentalist or stage magician also taps into their own inner psyche and uses a spiritual connection to read situations and people, or to distract with sleight of hand. They wouldn't appreciate me saying that though.

Consider this: electricity is a form of energy. We know it exists because we see the end result e.g. the TV, lights, vacuum cleaner etc. It cannot be created or destroyed, but it *can* be transformed. When making a prediction about a future event, or when we attempt to communicate with spirit, we're essentially transforming the energy of our mind. There are a number ways to do this and there is no right or wrong way to do it. You need to go with whatever works for you. I can't speak for other mediums, but for me a random and sudden thought placed into my mind by spirit tends to mean that I need to say or do something. I can almost guarantee that you were not thinking about a bowl of tomato soup until I gave you that thought. I can now suggest that you are now visualising that soup in your mind, steaming away and perhaps with a nice slice of chunky bread. That example of random thought processes is what you need to be aware of when working with spirit. It is how I know that a thought is my own, or given to me, more or less.

Many people believe that a medium goes around talking to the dead as if they can see and hear them as they do the living. Perhaps that's true for some, but it isn't how I work. There *have* been times when this has happened, but most of the time, I'm connecting to this universal energy and to the souls who are in reflection. It also means that those souls that never come through in a reading, or that never haunt the place they grew up, either don't feel the need to come through during their reflection, or they have already progressed and have been reborn.

This concept is a difficult one to master and so in this chapter, I'm going to break it down. If you wish to try and develop your own spiritual awareness, some of the information that I'm going to present may be helpful to you.

So, what exactly is *intuitive perception*?

Regardless of the method, most of the time it can be a combination of two or more things; I 'see' images in my mind, 'hear' conversations in my mind or experience something that I can best describe as déjà vu.

Before we talk about reading people (some of you may want know how this works so that you can try it for yourself), we need to discuss intuitive perception. You have likely heard that mediums work in different ways, typically clairvoyance is the most heard of method. Numerous spiritual philosophies contain the notion of an inner third eye that is related to the chakra system and to which is attributed significance in mystical awakening or enlightenment, clairvoyant perception, and higher states of consciousness. This idea occurs historically in ancient, central, and east Asia; and also in contemporary occult theories relating to yoga, Theosophy, Pagan religions, and New Age spiritual philosophies. The activity of the pineal gland is only partially understood. Its location deep in the brain suggested to philosophers throughout history that it possesses particular importance. This combination led to its being regarded as a "mystery" gland with mystical, metaphysical, and occult theories surrounding its perceived functions.

Typically, we all have five grounded senses that we use daily to include our sense of *sight*, *hearing*, *taste*, *touch* and *smell*. You'll have heard of the elusive sixth sense. Well, that's what I call intuitive perception. It doesn't exist by itself, but is fed by all your senses combined. And remember that human WiFi that I referred to previously? That also comes into play.

You need to understand some terminology before you continue. Intuitive perception (or your intuition) is based on what you think and feel at any given time. This may be as result of something in the physical world, or it could be as a result of something that you're experiencing spiritually.

Clairvoyance abilities allow us to 'see' images in our mind. For me, spirit communicate using signs and symbols that I can understand. Or they may show me an image that when described, has meaning for the person that I'm reading.

Clairaudience abilities allow one to 'hear' spirit talk. Although I have experienced this, it is not common for me and the ability to hear spirit voices is rare. At least, I'm not hearing them as I'd hear you talk to me. Instead, I'm 'hearing' the conversation in my mind. It's also worth pointing out that some spirit do not talk at all, like the man I met in the abandoned building when I was with Robert.

Clairsentience abilities allow us to feel things. We may feel that spirit is near us, or we may be empathic and feel emotions and thoughts. Have you ever visited a place, for example a potential new home, and upon entering you simply feel that it's wrong? Or you may have heard stories about people feeling that they're being watched, or that they're sad in a place where there has been a tragic event in the past.

Claircognisant abilities allow us to simply know things. This can be in foresight or in hindsight. For example, I often meet someone for the first time and I know something about them, without actually understanding how. Or I may think about someone and they then message me or they call me.

There are other abilities too, such as the ability to smell or feel spirit touch you. I've described other terms in a glossary at the end of this book. During a reading, I use all these abilities to connect to spirit. So, what does spirit communication look like? I'm going to talk you through a typical scenario where

I'm reading someone. Regardless of whether this is a private sitting, a charity floor show or a paranormal investigation, the process is the same. The only caveat being that the energy on location during an investigation does not feel the same as it does when I connect with loved ones during a reading. I have been known to pass on messages to people attending an investigation, but I normally keep this these two things separate. The main reason for this being: loved ones tell the truth and some interactions with spirit during an investigation are less truthful and less sincere. I do not believe in evil, but I do believe in human nature and our capacity to do evil things to each other. There are nasty spirits just as there are nasty people on this Earth.

In the reflection at the end of this chapter, I'll provide you with some techniques that may help you should you wish to develop your intuitive perception. I have also provided an entire chapter to raising your awareness of spirit, so I'll give you some things to think about there. For now, this is what goes through my head during an interaction.

I ask in my mind, for spirit to step forward. In doing so, I instinctively know that they're close as I can feel them. Sometimes, I'll see them as I see you, and at other times I feel heat, like a tingling sensation on the nape of my neck. This is my Spidey sense kicking in. I begin to ask them questions based on the information that they give to me. They all communicate differently, some using their voice, others using images and most using emotions and impressions. It's like having a conversation under water. You can see and hear things but they're distorted and surreal. So, I begin to probe deeper. I use various distraction techniques to communicate and to obtain information. As on this Earth plane, some give lots of information across and others don't. It's not unusual to simply feel the presence of someone, but other than a male, female, adult or child I cannot always tell for sure who I'm connected with.

In my mind, I now picture a dial or a gauge. It has male at one end and female at the other. I ask spirit to take the dial to one side or another.

Female. Ok, so I have a lady with me.

Are you alone?

The same dial, with different variable. *Yes.*

And so the pattern repeats. Changes come as I begin to ask more open ended questions, such as their name or the names of people connected to them. I can be hit and miss on names. Sometimes, I'm given many names, and at other times none. It's not something that can be forced from spirit. They either give you that information or they don't. This also applies to other information. It would be great if they came forward and told us everything about them, as Mark did that day in my office at the university. But life doesn't work like that and we need to build the bridges ourselves.

This is where your intuitive perception comes in. I've hosted many workshops over the years and as a qualified teacher, I'm grounded on learning outcomes and teaching design. I always tell people to trust in their instincts. But I also know that's a hard thing to do. I recall a charity event that I once hosted. I told a woman in the audience that her brother was beside her in spirit. I continued, by laughing when I said that he wanted her to know that he 'had his eye on her'. I knew there was a joke in this, but I didn't understand it. She told me afterwards that her brother was indeed in spirit and that he had a glass eye. He used to take it out and tell anyone willing to listen that he had his eye on them! This had come to me as those words had come to me without any consideration to them. It's like the soup, when information comes to me out of the blue, I know that spirit is giving it to me. This takes trust, both in spirit, your guides and in yourself.

I mentioned signs and symbols previously. When I work with spirit, and I need to get more information from them, I ask Harold to step forward and help me communicate with them. Typically, he will do this by showing me things that I can understand and later use to pass on a message. For example, a shield means protection, a compass means guidance and a black hand means a terminal illness.

I also take on characteristics of spirit, either their mannerisms, ways of talking or personality. This in itself can be good validation to someone, when they look startled and tell me, *"Oh my God, you sound just like my Dad!"*

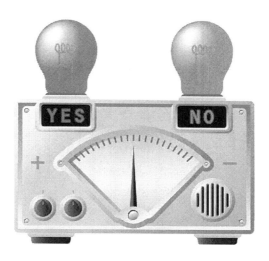

I try to visualise on my mind, dials and symbols that I can use when interacting with spirit. This one could be used when asking them Yes or No – closed questions.

END OF CHAPTER REFLECTION

Think about the signs and symbols that you would recognise if you were communicating with spirit. You don't need to reinvent the wheel as you'll already use many signs and symbols in your daily life. I've given you a list of what I use to get you started.

- A **compass** represents guidance
- A **shield** represents protection
- A **sword** represents a battle or a challenge
- A **black hand** represents a terminal illness
- **Pink** colours mean a girl or a female
- **Blue** colours mean a boy or a male (Blue can also mean communication as in the throat chakra – so these symbols need to be taken in context!)

Familiarise yourself with the chakra system and the associated colours as these may have significance when you communicate with spirit, e.g. the colour green may indicate the heart.

PARANORMAL INVESTIGATION

"Our physical and mental health is important and it can be too easy to compromise this by regular investigation that takes one too deep."

What do we actually mean by 'paranormal'? For some, this will invoke thoughts about hauntings, ghosts and poltergeist activity and all the things that you would have seen on TV. For others, it will include all that, as well as wider unknowns within the Universe. For example, alien visitations, connections to our ancient past, folklore and occurrences of the supernatural and extraordinary. The definition of paranormal, if referenced against *Wikipedia*, will tell you that *'events are purported phenomena described in popular culture, folk, and other non-scientific bodies of knowledge, whose existence within these contexts is described as beyond normal experience or scientific explanation.'*

The truth of the matter is, this is all correct. Essentially, the paranormal field is diverse and the eclectic mix of beliefs and experiences as well as the imagination of authors and script writers has resulted in a perverse fascination with the beyond – beyond this life and Earth plane and beyond time and space itself.

So what *is* real?

It's hard to answer that, as we are all on the spectrum of sceptic verses believer and we are all on various points of the spiritual scale (remember that first reflection that you carried out at the end of my Foreword?). That is, we tend to believe the things that we experience and we apply some degree of scepticism when others relay their stories of encounters with the unknown.

But that's ok.

Historically, people believed that the Earth was flat and that if they sailed too far, they would fall off the edge of the World. We might laugh at that now, but without a doubt, our descendants in a few hundred years will likely look back at us and think *how did they not know or understand?*

It was in the summer of 2013 when I decided to attend my first real paranormal investigation. It seems like a lifetime ago. Little did I know that it would set me on a path from which I could not turn.

Early experiences (especially the sinister energy from Madame Tussaud's) had tainted my opinion of the paranormal and I had actively tried to avoid locations reputed as haunted. At this time in my life, I had no real desire to expose myself to such energy. I was new to paranormal investigation, but not to *the* paranormal. At least, that's what I thought.

I was browsing the internet one evening and I stumbled upon a website promoting a paranormal investigation at Mains Castle in Dundee. Somehow, I felt that I needed to attend and Harold urged me to put aside my misgivings and give it a go. I mentioned it to Claire and she kicked the ball back into my court. It was entirely my decision to make, she told me. The night was crystal clear and the stars twinkled against the dark blue, evening sky. The sun was setting and I'd arrived early at the castle. I had already contacted the team running the event to tell them that I was a medium and I'd asked if they were okay with this.

Sadly, not all teams are open minded. Some focus solely on scientific investigation and that's fine. Likewise, some focus only on the spiritual aspects, and that's fine, too. I do believe, however, that in order to get the most out of an investigation, one needs to adopt various approaches and methodologies and maintain a degree of flexibility.

The diagram below illustrates my preferred stance towards paranormal investigation. I regularly promote triangulation of data sources, but in reality there are four categories that inform an evidence based approach.

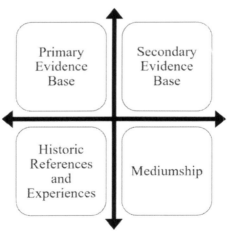

Figure 1: An evidence based approach.

Primary evidence provides the foundation for the scientific exploration of alleged activity. This can be data provided by audio, visual or other equipment, for example, the elusive phenomena captured on camera or electronic voice phenomenon (EVP).

Secondary evidence may be data provided by other investigation teams or by experts whom have previously been on location. It's always important to establish your own baseline data, but at the same time we shouldn't dismiss information that is readily available to us. This could be significant if there is later on, correlation of findings. Historic references (e.g. the recorded history of a building) and the experiences of people living in, working in or visiting the location provide another basis of information that can be useful to us. Eye witness accounts can be invaluable in trying to understand the type of haunting that may be taking place. Mediumship and the spiritual sensitivity of those attending the investigation concludes the triangulation. This makes for a cleaner approach to investigation, where we search internally: *What does my equipment tell me? What do others tell me? What does my own intuition tell me?*

It is this internal process that either makes us a sceptic or a believer. It's how we deal with information and it's how our own emotional intelligence and epistemologies govern our thought processes. Typically, a scientific investigator will favour their equipment, whereas a medium will favour their own senses. Someone new to investigation will likely rely on what others tell them. That's worth remembering when we invite guests along to a public investigation. It really annoys me when I see groups telling potential guests that a location is 'the most haunted' or that there is 'poltergeist activity' or even 'dark entities' in a fantastical and elaborate means to entice people into buying tickets for their 'scary' event. And don't get me started on the groups who have little interest in spirit and are simply out to make money. They give genuine investigators a bad reputation when things go wrong. I nearly attended an investigation at a [reputed] haunted castle in England in 2016. Imagine my surprise when I discovered it was £80 per ticket and that there were 100 tickets on sale!

What the f**k is that all about!? Could you imagine that many people cutting around trying to find a sign of spirit interaction? Ridiculous.

Luckily for me, that night at Mains Castle was genuine and the group I was with behaved in a way that was exemplary. The team opened the door to me and I was welcomed to the castle by their medium. She gave me one of the best pieces of advice ever given to me regarding the paranormal. I took this onboard, given that I knew I was about to expose myself to something that I'd actively avoided for many years.

"This place is jumping with spirit," she told me. "Don't go in bouncing or they'll drain your energy before you realise what's happening. You need to keep some of it to pace yourself through the night."

Spirit use our energy like a battery. When we ask them to do things during an investigation, that energy needs to come from somewhere. This is why equipment batteries tend to drain quickly. They can also do this to us, and mediums are even more open to such draining as our energy has a big pointy arrow that says *Get your free energy here – this person is open, willing and able to share!* We are the proverbial light to a moth.

Inside, the great hall was warm and cast in shadows, the source an open log fire burning at one end of the room. My Spidey sense was on full alert and I instinctively knew that spirit was present. I was in attendance with other guests and I wasn't working my mediumship at this stage. I had simply decided to go on the advice of Harold and I wanted to see what all the fuss was about. Little did I know that it would alter my life and open my eyes to the possibilities that spirit could and would communicate in many ways. There's something compelling about investigating alleged paranormal activity. Anyone whom has attended an investigation would likely tell you how addictive it can be and I've seen some people fall into an unhealthy obsession.

I know many who go too deep and seek answers about life and death through investigation, in relation to something dark or related to witchcraft. Not the sort of arts that modern day witches practice (I know many witches and they're not dark and moody as would be portrayed on the TV), but something sinister and almost demonic. We need to be careful that we don't investigate at the expense of our energy. Physical and mental health is important and it can be too easy to compromise this by regular investigation that takes one too deep into the unseen world. I always advise people to maintain a tether to reality – a spiritual safety rope that grounds you to your life beyond paranormal investigation. When one becomes tired or too immersed, they open themselves to negative energy and attachments. As in all things in life, things need to come in balance.

That evening, as I moved around the castle and as I engaged in various experiments, I felt Harold stay close to me, all the time providing me with names, details and information. In my head, I was engaged in conversation with him as he revealed things about the spirit that we interacted with. It felt natural and I knew after that night that this was something that I needed to do. I didn't intend to use my mediumship openly, but that's exactly what happened. I began to speak out and tell people in the group what I could see and hear. The more that I spoke, the more activity we seemed to get.

On location at Mains Castle in Dundee, Scotland, telling people what I could sense via my mediumship. This was my first paranormal investigation.

The 3am Club was founded in June 2014 with our first investigation taking place at Scotland Street School and Museum in the September. This was an exciting time and we found ourselves to be really busy within a matter of weeks. I was still working at the university at this time and through my work there I met Peter, who was the Director of the first ever Scottish Paranormal Festival. The Festival took place over four days (Thursday to Sunday) and included a range of activities and talks. The 3am Club was invited to conduct three investigations on the Thursday, Friday and Saturday nights and to facilitate a workshop presentation on investigation methods on the Saturday afternoon. This was a big deal as it drew thousands of tourists from all over the world and our event tickets quickly sold out.

Our engagement with the Festival was a huge success. We investigated the Darnley Coffee House on our first night. It's located at the top of Stirling Town Centre and it has a reputation as being haunted. It had never been investigated before. From there, we then moved onto an investigation granted by permission from Stirling Council, who allowed us to venture beneath the Thistle Shopping Centre after the doors had closed. Our final evening concluded with an investigation at Cowane's Hospital. Interestingly, during the event, we were joined by a local medium from Stirling. I was amazed and pleased when independently, we could sense the same spirits trying to interact with the group.

An original advert for the Scottish Paranormal Festival, (2014).

Over the years I've lost count on the number of places that I've investigated. I've been to many locations more than once and would estimate that I've attended 150+ investigations. The list below isn't exhaustive but it does provide an illustration on the places where I've been, either by myself or as a member of a team. It does not include investigations conducted in private homes and residences or those whereby I simply visited in the passing.

- Mains Castle, Scotland.
- Castle Menzies, Scotland.
- Scotland Street School and Museum, Scotland.
- The Secret Bunker, Scotland.
- World War II Aircraft Hanger, Scotland.
- Niddry Street Vaults, Scotland.
- Bannockburn House, Scotland.
- Culross Palace, Scotland.
- Plane Castle, Scotland.
- Cowane's Hospital, Scotland.
- Stirling Old Town Jail, Scotland.

- Bo'ness Town Hall, Scotland.

- Stirling Castle, Scotland.

- Sauchie Tower, Scotland.

- Broomhall Castle, Scotland.

- Darnley Coffee House, Scotland.

- Stirling Arcade, Scotland.

- Stirling Thistle Centre and Bastion, Scotland.

- Smith Museum, Scotland.

- The Town House, Scotland.

- Merchants House, Scotland.

- Sailors Walk, Scotland.

- Gargunnock House, Scotland.

- Castle Menzies, Scotland.

- The Swan Inn, Scotland.

- The Bucklyvie Inn, Scotland.

- Rob Roy Cottage, Scotland.

- Lead Mining Museum, Scotland.

- Provanhall House, Scotland.

- Balgonie Castle, Scotland.

- Invarary Jail, Scotland.

- Tower of Hallbar, Scotland.

- The Tall Ship, Scotland.

- RSS Discovery, Scotland.

- Gilmerton Cove, Scotland.

- Dunmore House, Scotland.

- Torwood Castle, Scotland.

- Pittenweem Tower, Scotland.

- The Fisheries Museum, Scotland.

- Alton Towers, England.

- Thackray Medical Museum and Asylum, England.

- Bundoora Homestead, Australia.

- Painted Churches and Monasteries, Romania.

- Ancient Crypts, Romania.

- Churches and Roman Ruins, Bulgaria.

On location (and dressed up!) at the Secret Bunker, Fife, Scotland.

As a medium, I know all too well the dangers when investigating spiritual interaction. I've come under psychic attack on many occasions. From a headache, to seeing the flashing red eyes of an elemental, the scariest form of attack happens when I channel spirit directly. This occurs when spirit energy intersects with my own. I use a technique called tunneling, which is where I visualise myself standing at the end of a long tunnel. Furthest away from me is a bright light. I 'see' spirit standing in the light and as they walk closer to me, their features and details become clearer in my mind. If they get too close they begin to channel through me. I've done this through invitation in the past (in a controlled environment) but now and again they 'jump' me and take over. Some people would call this possession, but it is not possession, at least not in the biblical sense. Rather, they speak through me, using my voice, or they are able to control my movements. This is draining and leaves me very tired. Normally, it only lasts for a few minutes and then the energy wears out, or Harold steps in and breaks the connection.

One of the most memorable times was again, at Mains Castle. There is a little man in spirit in the castle. He would have been a jester or some sort of entertainer. His name is Hector. He once channeled through me and his delight was obvious to all who witnessed this. He was very funny. Oddly, at times I have spoken with strange accents and even in foreign tongue. I do not speak any other languages (at least not fluently) but I've been known to cite Latin. Some mediums who can channel open their eyes when channeling, and remain able to walk and behave normally. The rhythm and the intonation of the voice may also change completely. I have friends who can channel in different ways, with some writing backwards (in the dark) and some taking onboard the emotions of spirit without realising what is going on.

Channeling spirit on location at Pittenweem Tower, Scotland. This was a particularly nasty man in spirit, determined to let his voice be heard.

It's important not to lose perspective when investigating an alleged haunting. It's easy to mistake simple occurrences as spiritual activity. We need to promote an evidence based approach; that is we use a variety of equipment and resources to capture information and data and if it can't be explained then it *might* just be supernatural. This is what I illustrated in my triangulation matrix.

Mediumship enhances the experience throughout an investigation. When science meets spiritualism, then we know that we have a case to present. The two must work together to provide an overall impression of a location. I always try to triangulate data to form information which tells us what type of haunting may be occurring, what experiences are common and what may be happening within a location. The triangulation of data comes from eye witness accounts, client experiences, mediumship and clinical evidence bases (captured by equipment).

Anecdotal evidence such as those captured through personal experiences lack the rigor of empirical evidence and is not amenable to scientific investigation. The anecdotal approach is not a scientific approach to the paranormal because it leaves verification dependent on the credibility of the party presenting the evidence. It is also subject to cognitive bias, inductive reasoning and other fallacies that may prevent the anecdote from having meaningful information to impart. Nevertheless, it is a common approach to paranormal phenomena and should not be easily dismissed. After all, some of the best evidence in my mind, has been the multiple witness accounts presented to me, which could not be easily explained away.

Charles Fort (1874 – 1932) is perhaps the best known collector of paranormal anecdotes. Fort is said to have compiled as many as 40,000 notes on unexplained phenomena, though there were no doubt many more than these. These notes came from what he called *"the orthodox conventionality of Science"*, which were odd events originally reported in magazines, respected newspapers such as The Times and respected mainstream scientific journals such as Scientific American, Nature and Science. From his research, he wrote seven books, though only four are known to have survived. These are: The Book of the Damned (1919), New Lands (1923), Lo! (1931) and Wild Talents (1932).

His interests included teleportation (a term Fort is generally credited with coining); poltergeist events, falls of frogs, fishes, inorganic materials of an amazing range; crop circles; unaccountable noises and explosions; spontaneous fires; levitation; ball lightning (a term explicitly used by Fort); unidentified flying objects; mysterious appearances and disappearances; giant wheels of light in the oceans; and animals found outside their normal habitats. He offered many reports of OOP Arts, abbreviation for "out of place" artifacts: strange items found in unlikely locations. He also is perhaps the first person to explain strange human appearances and disappearances by the hypothesis of alien abduction, and was an early proponent of the extraterrestrial hypothesis. Fort is considered by many as the father of modern paranormalism, which is the study of paranormal phenomena.

Although parapsychology has its roots in earlier research, it began using the experimental approach in the 1930s under the direction of J. B. Rhine (1895 – 1980). Rhine popularised the now famous methodology of using card-guessing and dice-rolling experiments in a laboratory in the hopes of finding a statistical validation of extra-sensory perception (ESP). I've used these techniques in spiritual awareness workshops with various degrees of success. I have my doubts that they present an accurate perspective on psychic ability. That expected ability is born from our experiences of the TV and from books and doesn't reflect the reality of mediumship.

In 1957, the Parapsychological Association was formed as the preeminent society for parapsychologists. In 1969, they became affiliated with the American Association for the Advancement of Science. That affiliation, along with a general openness to psychic and occult phenomena in the 1970s, led to a decade of increased parapsychological research. During this time, other notable organisations were also formed, including the Academy of Parapsychology and Medicine (1970), the Institute of Parascience (1971), the Academy of Religion and Psychical Research, the Institute for Notec Sciences (1973), and the International Kirlian Research Association (1975). Each of these groups performed experiments on paranormal subjects to varying degrees. Parapsychological work was also conducted at the Stanford Research Institute during this time.

With the increase in parapsychological investigation, there came an increase in opposition to both the findings of parapsychologists and the granting of any formal recognition of the field. Criticisms of the field were focused in the founding of the Committee for the Scientific Investigation of Claims of the Paranormal (1976), now called the Committee for Skeptical Inquiry, and its periodical, Skeptical Inquirer [nee:sceptical].

As astronomer Carl Sagan put it, *"extraordinary claims require extraordinary evidence"*, and experimental research into the paranormal continues today, though it has waned considerably since the 1970s. One such experiment is called the Ganzfeld Experiment. The purpose of the Ganzfeld Experiment, like other parapsychological experiments, is to test for statistical anomalies that might suggest the existence of psi, a process indicating psychic phenomena. In the Ganzfeld Experiment, a subject (receiver) is asked to access through psychic means, some target.

The target is typically a picture or video clip selected randomly from a large pool, which is then viewed in a remote location by another subject (sender). Ganzfeld experiments use audio and visual sensory deprivation to remove any kind of external stimulus that may interfere with the testing or corrupt the test by providing cues to correct targets. A 'hit' refers to a correctly identified target. The expected hit ratio of such a trial is 1 in 4, or 25%. Deviations from this expected ratio might be seen as evidence for psi, although such conclusions are often disputed. To date there have been no experimental results that have gained wide acceptance in the scientific community as valid evidence of paranormal phenomena.

As such, I always go into an investigation with an open mind, though grounded in looking for natural explanations. This is a natural response and is the basis for Occam's razor. Since standard scientific models generally predict what can be expected in the natural world, the debunking approach presumes that what appears to be paranormal is necessarily a misinterpretation of natural phenomena, rather than an actual anomalous phenomenon. In contrast to the sceptical position, which requires claims to be proven, the debunking approach actively seeks to disprove the claims. It's not a term that I like, and I don't use it often. To me, these are one extreme to another. I would encourage a contemporary investigator to position themselves on the fence in all matters. Oddly, even as a medium, this is my default position.

Former stage magician, James Randi, is a well-known debunker of paranormal claims and a prominent member of a group of sceptics. As a sceptic with a background in illusion, Randi feels that the simplest explanation for those claiming paranormal abilities is trickery, illustrated by demonstrating that the spoon bending abilities of psychic Uri Geller can easily be duplicated by trained magicians. He is also the founder of the James Randi Educational Foundation and its famous million dollar challenge offering a prize of USD $1,000,000 to anyone who can demonstrate evidence of any paranormal, supernatural or occult power or event, under test conditions agreed to by both parties.

An alternative to debunking is found in the field of anomalistic. Anomalistic differs from debunking in that debunking works on the premise that something is either a misidentified instance of something known to science, or that it is a hoax, while anomalistic works on the premise that something may be either of the above, or something that can be rationalised using an as yet unexplored avenue of science.

By immersing oneself in the subject being studied, a researcher is presumed to gain understanding of the subject. In paranormal research, a participant-observer study might consist of a researcher visiting a place where alleged paranormal activity is said to occur and recording observations while there.

As a medium, it can be too easy to be pulled in different directions, depending on the default stance that one takes towards investigation. One of the most common reasons for someone to contact me is where they feel that they're being haunted, or someone has had a frightening experience and they're looking for some guidance. Not all investigations are in public buildings and many of my best memories are actually from the time that I've spent in private residences.

So, what can you do if you think you're haunted? First, it's essential that you understand that 90% of suspected hauntings and paranormal activity have logical explanations. Any genuine activity is normally benign - it is very rare to experience poltergeist or malicious activity. Before you contact a medium or a paranormal investigation team, I recommend that you follow this advice. Buy yourself a notebook and maintain a journal or diary. This is important as it helps us to ascertain any patterns. You should consider the following questions and write down answers to them as they occur.

1) What activity are you/others experiencing?

2) What makes you think it is paranormal?

3) Where are you experiencing the activity? Your home or place of work? Is it isolated to one specific area?

4) Did the activity start suddenly (if so - when?) or has it gradually worsened?

5) Who is affected? Who is experiencing activity?

6) Have you taken steps to rule out logic?

7) Have you changed anything in the house?

8) Have you introduced anything new to the house (that is old e.g. jewellery or second-hand furniture?).

9) When is the activity? In your diary, record any experiences and note the date and time.

10) Try to find out something about the location - the building's history or was there something built

on the land previously?

11) Are there any animals in the building and have they been acting strange?

12) Are there any children under the age of 16 in the house and are they aware of suspected activity? Are they frightened by their experiences?

13) Are you curious about suspected activity or do you feel a sense of threat?

14) Have you been able to capture any 'evidence' of suspected activity? Or are these personal experiences? Has more than one person experienced the same activity?

15) Record anything else in your journal that you feel may be relevant and appropriate.

I suggest that you complete the journal over a (minimum) two week period as in many instances, activity can start and then end over the period of a few weeks and it may never happen again. Once you have done this, and you feel that more action / investigation is required, it's time to escalate to a more knowledgeable other. These questions can also form the basis for an investigation. I regularly reflect on them when I'm asked to help someone who believes that they are being haunted.

I'm often asked if I believe in angels and demons, heaven and hell. In short, the answer is *I don't know – probably not*. The reason for this is simple, even if the rationale is more complex. I've never encountered a demonic entity in my forty years on this Earth, nor have I encountered an angel. To believe in angels and demons requires one to also have a religious grounding in their belief system. I've already declared my stance on this. I neither believe in God nor do I disbelieve in Him. I do believe in my own experiences and that includes spirit, and the masters who guide us. That said, I have encountered spirit that has never taken human form. I call them elementals. These typically take form from earth, fire, water or air and they are captured in folklore as sprites, fairies, pixies, trolls, leprechauns and so forth. I suspect (strongly) that many mistake these forms of spiritual energy as demons, for they can be scary and often attack people psychically. But they are extremely rare. I have only ever encountered three.

It was February, 2015 when I agreed to stay over at a 16th Century Tower House near Glasgow. I arrived with my team on the Friday evening. The snow had been falling and as the car swept down the access road, the Tower was illuminated in the glow of a street lamp. It looked like a scene from the *Chronicles of Narnia – The Lion, The Witch and the Wardrobe*. The Tower was built over four levels, with a kitchen located on the ground floor, the great hall on level one and the bedrooms on level two and three. The fourth level took one out onto the roof, where a further bedroom was located in the attic space. This was to be my room. There was no outside phone line, but the rooms each had an internal phone in them, so that you could call from one room to the next for convenience. The floors were connected with steep, stone steps built into the walls. I recall how unfit I was, and it took my breath from me moving from one level to the next.

The evening started well. As we all arrived, we

settled in and lit the open fire. Over a homemade dinner, we dined and laughed in anticipation of the investigation, which we decided we'd do on the Saturday night. It was around 10.00pm when we thought it would be a good idea to have a walk around. So we opened up and I placed protection onto everyone.

The steep, stone steps were built into the wall space. It took a lot of effort to move from one level to the next.

That's when things started to go wrong. Harold was giving me warning signs and telling me that the things I was experiencing (from my mediumship) was smoke and mirrors. Everyone in attendance was experiencing something different. I felt uneasy and I knew something wasn't right, but I couldn't put my finger on it, so we carried on. We ventured up to the third level bedrooms and sat in the dark, calling out to see if anything would happen.

The phone started to ring. We all jumped as this was not expected. Everyone was in the same room and the phone lines were internal only. How could it be ringing out? After much debate, one of us picked up the call, only for everyone to hear a sinister growl on the other end. The phone slammed down and we started to worry. By now we had shared our concerns with each other, and we thought it would be a good idea to take a break. Everyone retired to the open fire and the heat in the great hall, with exception to myself and one other. We volunteered to go down to the kitchen to make tea and coffee.

Now, you need to understand that although I'm a

serious person, I actually have a sense of humour that is very unique. With a laugh, I picked up the phone and told my companion that I was going to call the bedroom back, knowing fine well that everyone else was in the great hall. To my amazement, the phone line was engaged. Puzzled, I put the receiver down, only for it to start ringing! Of course, I dared not pick it up again. *Note: we later asked the building manager if there were any known issues with the phone system – he told us that there were in perfect working order!*

We were all spooked by this stage. We called it a night and went to bed. I washed up in the bathroom and climbed the steps to the fourth level bedroom. It was a terrible sleep. I awakened at around 4am to find a woman sat on the bottom of my bed. She was around twenty years old and had her hair up in a bun. She stared at me intently, and just as quickly as I became aware of her, she was gone. I tried to get back to sleep, but my dreams were disturbed with sounds of running water (there was a stream outside the Tower), and children crying.

Shattered, I went downstairs for breakfast. Beside the Tower was a cottage. Two friends had slept there, and they also had experienced a restless night. One of them believed that she had been awakened by a wet tongue of an animal licking her face. Yuck!

The day came and went and the full investigation had started. As we moved around the building, Harold began to describe to me a small man around 4 foot in height. He had wooden teeth and he liked to carve up meat. He shown me an image of leathers and skins hanging up to dry. I didn't like the sound of this at all. The Ouija board was in use at the time and it started to present us with the name of a known demon. Harold stepped in and told me to stop and to close down the investigation. It is one of few times that I have ever felt the need to do so. I told the others how I felt and we all agreed that enough was enough. We packed up the equipment and went back to the Tower. The door had been locked and no one had been inside for the past two hours, so imagine how we felt when we went inside and discovered wet footprints on the stone steps leading from the kitchen to the great hall. This was not natural.

Scared, and although we were seasoned investigators, we all slept together that night, in the great hall.

It was a few days afterwards when I relived the experience with a demonologist from the US. He had been a friend on Facebook for a few years and I decided to share my experience with him. I had my doubts about demons and such like, but I was intrigued with what he had to say, as I felt that I had encountered something that wasn't human. He began to tell me that what we had encountered had all the markings of an elemental. He told me that in the days gone by, it was quite common for builders to invoke elementals as a form of protection, ironically to ward off evil spirits and enemies of the families who inhabited the buildings. Could the short man with the wooden teeth have been a troll or similar elemental energy?

I hadn't felt right for the past two weeks. I was off work with a serious lack of energy, the shakes and with a nervous disposition. I recall bathing in warm water and thinking to myself that something had come home with me from that Tower. I decided to cleanse my chakras and perform some self-healing. I told Harold to help rid anything negative from within my own energy field, and as I did so I felt the need to throw up. Leaning over the toilet, I sicked up a thick, black liquid. As soon as it left my body, I felt right again. The change within me was instantaneous. I had an attachment. It was another lesson for me in spiritual protection and in the absolute need to regularly cleanse my aura. I featured at the time in *Chat It's Fate* magazine and they decided to run with the story from the Tower. Much to my dismay, they ran with the headline *I Sicked up a Spirit*, though my friends within the paranormal world of investigation thought this was hilarious.

END OF CHAPTER REFLECTION

Here are some techniques for you to reflect on when you're next on location, either during an investigation or even out and about visiting an old building.

- ✓ Imagine spirit walking towards you in a tunnel.
- ✓ If you can't see anyone, it may mean that spirit is not stepping forward to you. Invite them to do this (make sure you've opened up and protected yourself, first!).
- ✓ Ask them to show their face to you, or to give you a name or other detail about themselves.
- ✓ Think about how you feel– are you happy, scared, upset etc.
- ✓ Invite them to come close to you and to do something to show that they are present – I always invite them to place images into my mind, to speak so that I may hear them or to let themselves be known.

✓ Remember that the best interactions come when you least expect it. You're more likely to see spirit (either a full apparition or a shadow) when you're moving around from one room to another and not really thinking about them – this is why distraction techniques are helpful. Try thinking happy thoughts – being abusive and negative towards them rarely works – instead be respectful, open and honest.

FEAR AND COURAGE

"Even the best of us are tested at times. We all have lessons to learn so that our souls may advance and grow, and it's frustrating when we can't easily see what those lessons are."

One of the most heartfelt aspects of my work as a medium are the stories that I hear from the people that I meet. People from all walks of life and from diverse backgrounds tend to come to me for a reading and I previously mentioned possible reasons; they wish to connect with a loved one in spirit, they need guidance in their life and want to know what's ahead, or they're curious about the afterlife and are seeking some form of enlightenment, or perhaps even entertainment. You would be surprised with some of the stories that I could tell you. They're all equally profound in their own way and they're unique to everyone associated with them.

I'm an advocate for supporting positive mental health. I occasionally come across someone who is really struggling with life. Usually, they wear a mask of pretence. That is, on the outside it appears that they're coping, but on the inside there's a sea of turmoil and chaos. This leads to confusion that in extreme circumstances can lead to attempted suicide. Occasionally, the attempt is successful. Let me be clear, these souls do not become lost nor do they become placed in purgatory. Rather, they enter reflection as do other souls. Death does not differentiate between us, in the way that we die. Life is very binary. You're either alive or you're not. There's no half way in between, though it often feels like it and there are times when we have one foot in this world and one in the next, but physically the body still lives.

It was in August 2014 when I was out and about at the local shops in my home town. I'd just picked up some items from a store when I needed to cross the road to go to the bank. As I was standing at the kerbside, a young woman around 25 years of age moved up beside me. I noticed the shine in her black hair and the contrast in her red coat. We stood there in silence for a few minutes, waiting for a gap to appear in the traffic. To this day, I have no idea what actually happened, or where the message had come from, but I reached out to her and placed my hand on her arm. She jumped in surprise but didn't pull away from me, her eyes meeting mine for what seemed like an eternity but was actually seconds.

"Your mum loves you very much," I said. "And she says that she'll never forgive you if you do it."

There it was. I'd said it. The words had weighed on me and I simply couldn't contain them. Without thinking, they came out in a flood of emotion as I reached out to her. She stood staring at me blankly, her expression flicking from surprise to something else that I couldn't easily read. In that moment, I turned and walked back the way that I'd come, leaving her dumbfounded, by herself at the edge of the road. I dared not to look back and the panic started to set in with the realisation on what I'd done. I quickly found my parked car and made a hasty retreat home, convinced that I would have been caught on CCTV and that the Police would be calling for me. Of course, they never did arrive. After a few days, I forgot about the incident and life had moved on. Around three weeks later, I received a message on social media. The young woman had found me. Apparently, my message to her that day had had a major impact on her life and she had made enquiries, and had thus discovered who I was and what I do.

"Hi, there. Sorry for the random message, are you the man who does readings?" she asked.

"Yes, that's me," I replied.

"Not sure if you'll remember, but you gave me a message in the street a few weeks ago. Sorry if it wasn't you. I had asked some friends and they said it probably was and you look the same from your profile picture."

"Yes, that was me," I said, wondering where this was going. I knew exactly who she was.

"Ah, cool. I wanted to speak to you. I'm needing a reading and you said something that had a real impact on me."

Shit. I've landed myself in it now, I thought to myself.

"Oh, I'm sorry about that. I don't make a habit of stopping people at random and passing on messages." I explained. "It does happen now and again, though. I apologise if I upset you or caused offence."

I waited for what seemed like forever as the little 'activity' dots bopped up and down to show that she was writing a reply. After a few minutes it came through.

"Not at all. I wanted to find you to say thanks. My mum died a few months ago and I've been really struggling with things. I don't have any family left and I'm by myself."

"Oh, I'm sorry to hear that," I said.

"I don't know why I need to get this off my chest but I feel I can be honest with you. I was thinking about suicide that day you stopped me. If I hadn't met you in the street, I might not be here, now."

And there it was.

Now the exact words my differ, but that conversation sentiment is as exact as my memory will recall. It was a lesson for me in that stage of my mediumship, that spirit can come to us and pass on messages when we least expect it. I don't need to be sitting down to 'read' someone when a message pops through. You will have read from my previous chapters that mediumship is a state of mind, and that one can communicate with spirit through that mindset, using signs, symbols and other distraction techniques. But that all said, there are times when something else is happening. Something that goes beyond intuitive perception and sits firmly in the hands of a high power, as if we're guided in that moment by an intellect that we're not aware of at the time. It's both inspiring and frightening at the same time.

This young woman was not the first I'd experienced such a connection with and she wasn't the last. Over the years, I would pass on many other messages at random. It's not something that I do as habit as you never know how the recipient will react. I've also been known to pick up on loved ones in spirit when out and about on paranormal investigations and there are many other stories that demonstrate fear and hope. But we also need to consider courage, and how our own beliefs can be challenged when something we experience contradicts the way that we genuinely think, or want to live our lives. For example, when we're tested in matters of relationships, finance and work. The hardest of all comes through matters of ill-health, with no differentiation between physical health and mental health. I have no doubt that as you read this, you'll be able to relate to at least one person you know, recognising the issues at hand.

One of my dearest friends is a fiercely proud and independent woman in her 50s. She's experienced many things in life and she walks a spiritual path to self-discovery and enlightenment. She's not religious in the traditional sense, but she does have a strong sense of self and she relates to efficacy in matters of healing and intuitive perception. Her ultimate test started a few years ago, when she experienced a series of family bereavements in close succession, first her mother and then a younger family member within weeks of each other, having already lost her brother to suicide 14 years earlier. These were extremely challenging times for

Caroline and for her family, yet her commitment to them masked deeper concerns around her health, for she was diagnosed after her mother's passing with breast cancer, and only recently this year diagnosed with a benign brain tumour. These are not the first interactions with the health service for she had not long undergone surgery to repair damage to her shoulder, which in itself took much longer to heal than first expected. The cancer diagnosis came as a blow at a time in her life when she should have been putting up her feet and enjoying the fruits of her hard work. Indeed, the real test was just beginning.

I've used her as an example of courage. She wouldn't appreciate me saying that she was especially courageous and she certainly wouldn't agree with me that spirit allowed her to maintain courage and hope. But she will tell you about the fear that it imparts to oneself and to those around us. Perhaps this has been realised in the longer term, but there were dark days awaiting for her from the moment the specialist identified the cancer. Now, there's something you need to understand about

Caroline. She is not the sort of person that bends easily to convention nor is she the sort of person who would simply take at face value the guidance and advice of medical practitioners, just because the advice they provide was 'the norm'. She engaged in her own research around her health matters and with a dogged determination, decided that radiation and chemotherapy for the cancer was not the course of action that she wanted to pursue. Caroline *only* agreed to a tablet that would help shrink the tumour, which then made it possible for surgery to remove it. Don't get me wrong. For many, these would be exactly the right [advised] treatments to follow, but for Caroline she decided to follow a holistic and therapeutic path for both the cancer and to shrink the brain tumour. This was not an easy choice to follow as she regularly sought signs and assurance from spirit that she was supported, even if life would continue to throw curve balls at her along the way, questioning everything that she experienced. But the approach worked for her, and continues to work. She has been pronounced cancer free from the doctors. She did not hide the fact from oncologists that she had chosen to take the holistic approach and now tries to help others see that there are other alternatives than taking the allopathic approach, which she believes can have debilitating and long term affects on the body. Her journey had been one of realisation and grief, not knowing if it would work. For three years, her life would be on hold as she sought to reconcile the person she once was, with the person she had become. In her darkest hour, she lashed out at the people around her and I recall the day that she told me it had made her an angry person.

Even the best of us are tested at times. We all have lessons to learn so that our souls may advance and grow and it's frustrating when we can't easily see what those lessons are. For many, we won't know until the day that we die. Poor health does not just impact on the individual, but also on the people around them. Souls live and learn together, and so lessons may be shared rather than singular. When we're born into this world our life experiences are matched to other souls whereby they need to be 'in the same boat' as us, or perhaps on the periphery of an experience. Remember that finely woven tapestry – you can see the image on the surface but turn it around and you'll also find many interwoven threads and connections that bind it all together.

For Caroline, as she began to see real dividends in her health, she began to experience other problems. The constant barrage and testing, both in the real world medical sense as well as in the philosophical sense would continue as she was moved from one specialist to another, never quite knowing exactly what was wrong with her or what it meant for the short, medium or longer term. The uncertainty leaves us with a loss of hope and without direction. We feel at the mercy of the universe – a profound abandonment in that despite our best efforts, dreams and aspirations, we can't do anything about the situations around us.

We all control our actions and behaviours and through our mindset, we can visualise happiness, good health and fortune. I'm a great believer in the law of attraction and the use of positivity to bring things into our life as we need them. We can all divide the things in our life into two categories – the things we like and the things we don't like. Once we've done that, we determine the great things around us (including the people) and we can begin to focus on the aspects where we need systemic change. We need to be careful in what we wish for, as spirit has a funny sense of humour. For example, if we asked for lots of money, we may find that we come across 100 pennies – so instead we need to be specific on what we ask for. Once we've asked for it, we can then let the universe do the rest, but we do need to be patient as it may not all come to us at once. Instead, spirit may present us with opportunities to realise our ask. This is typical when we ask for something connected to work or promotion. We may ask for more responsibility or more pay and spirit may bring to your attention the opportunity, but it's for you to decide if you put in your application or not. Spirit will guide and show you outcomes, but we are the ones who control the direction of our life, as it's through our decisions that our soul learns from the experiences around us.

Caroline and I have had many discussions on such matters. If you think that life is unfair and that there is a lack of equity, then you're right. We cannot control the actions and behaviours of other people nor can we directly control the situations around us, but we can control our reaction, internal thought processes and our mindset.

Not long after I started to read people, a teenager arrived at my door. She had asked me for a reading a few weeks earlier and I'd agreed. Back then, I conducted them in my house. My wife and children had moved themselves upstairs and in she came. The reading progressed and her mother had come through from the Higher Side of Life. It was around half way through the reading when I explained that I didn't feel as though her mum had been in spirit long. She started to cry and proceeded to tell me that I was right. Her mother had passed only two days before! If I'd known that at the time, I would never have given her a reading. I don't believe there's a rule that suggests spirit can't come through within the first 6 months of passing (a belief that I've heard many times), as I've seen them even as they have one foot in this world and one in the next. If anything, it's more to do with raw emotions and for the person to be ready to receive messages. *It's about their mindset – not spirit!* But the timing was meant to be, she told me. She knew her mum was about to die from terminal cancer and that the end was near, and so she had booked the reading. At the time, it was to seek comfort that other family members in spirit would collect her soul and carry her to the Higher Side. However, at it would turn out her mum died before we had the chance to talk about it. We conversed for longer than required, exploring the messages that her mum put forward through me. It was as she prepared to leave, I told her that her mum wanted her to take an umbrella to the funeral. An odd thing to say, but anyone whom has received a reading from me will tell you that I do get some odd things. It's these little things that later have importance to us. She reached out to me a few week later. She had attended the funeral, which had been the event that she had hoped it would be, with many people participating in their respects. It had been a beautiful sunny day, but remembering the message she carried her umbrella with her. Later, at the graveside, she was the only one to remain dry as the weather turned and the rain poured down. In that moment, mixed with the sad reality on the loss of her mum, this young lady stood in the realisation that she had been with her that day, and that even now she was still looking out for her daughter.

You'll see why I decided to call this chapter Fear and Courage. These are natural reactions to the situations around us and we need to understand our emotions as well as the emotions of the people that we care for. This intelligence forms an empathy. It's an intrinsic element of human WiFi.

Caroline still continues to battle ill-health, but the cancer has come and gone. She's a real fighter and isn't easily beaten. Her principles and epistemological beliefs have guided her, as did her spirituality when she needed it most.

She is still working to understand the lessons that she needed to learn, but in doing so her lessons become ours in that we have a better understanding about such matters because she's allowed me to share her story with you. It serves us to remember, that even in the darkest hour, there is light within each of us. This light exists within the people we love and forms a bond to guide us back onto the right path. So my message to you in reading this is simple. It's okay to be fearful and it's okay to feel a sense of helplessness. You're not unique when you feel low or when you feel that life has given up on you, BUT you must keep going. Life NEVER gives up on us, it's only our mindset that creates that illusion. Equally, you're loved and even if you feel lonely, you're not. ALWAYS remember that your soul is learning. Tomorrow is always a new day. We're allowed to make mistakes. Where there is fear, we can always find courage. Be the person that you need to be, or the person that you want to be, and not the person that everyone expects you to be. *That* is the key to happiness.

END OF CHAPTER REFLECTION

Looking after our mental health is as equally important as looking after our physical health. Here are some resources that I recommend you use. They may also be helpful if you're going to support someone you care about when they're experiencing a hard time in life.

SAMH (Scottish Association for Mental Health)

www.samh.org.uk

Samaritans

www.samaritans.org

MIND

www.mind.org.uk

Mental Health Foundation

www.mentalhealth.org.uk

IT'S OKAY NOT TO BE OKAY!

YOUR SPIRITUAL AWARENESS

"Don't be afraid to make mistakes. We are all human and contrary to belief, we are permitted to get things wrong now and again."

Typically, children and young adults have a greater awareness of spirit as they are less 'educated' and tend to apply less logic than adults. As we grow older, our brain takes over and most of us will dismiss the connections and signs that we're given. The smallest occurrences can go unnoticed and even occurrences that I'd call significant, such as the sighting of spirit form or their manifestation can be dismissed as a figment of the imagination.

I always advise people to ask out loud if they think they've just experienced something spiritual. To ask who it is and what they want, and to ask for another sign (remember to describe something specific). Some really great mediums don't develop their ability to work with spirit until they're much older. Although I experienced things from an early age, I was 30 years old before I really developed my ability beyond the natural awareness that I was born with. It's one thing to experience spirit, it's something else to be able to interpret what you experience and pass on messages to others living on this Earth plane. That takes practice and it takes a lot of patience. Mediumship is often described as a gift. True, it does come more naturally to some than others, but I believe that in time, we can all learn how to communicate with spirit. If you wish to develop and strengthen your own awareness and connection with them, I advise you to take the following steps.

Attend your local Spiritualist Church. You may be lucky and receive a message from the visiting medium, but at the very least it will let you feel the communion of spirit. This is a world in which you will need to immerse yourself. Look to see how mediums work, what they do and how they pass messages across to their audience. I'm not suggesting that you copy their style or approach as we're all unique, so you'll see differences in how we do things, but you may need to try a few things out before you find something that works for you.

Churches tend to offer development circles, too. They can provide guidance and a safe environment to try things out. You won't be judged unfairly and most people affiliated with the Church will laugh *with* you when you make a mistake, rather than laugh *at* you. They'll cry with you *when* you cry and they'll push you in the right direction. Remember though, to always protect yourself when working with spirit. Most Churches will incite some form of protection, but not all of them.

There are many types of mediumship and I've described them throughout this book. You don't need to aspire to appear on the stage as a platform medium, but you may want to read a few people now and again. You only need to look on *Facebook* to find there are loads of mediums and psychics putting themselves forward. It's a brave thing to do in a society that still sees spiritualism as taboo, fraudulent or egotistical. Do what feels right to you and do what you're comfortable with. If you're meant to be on platform, then spirit will guide you to that. Physical mediumship such as transfiguration and the channelling of energy is a difficult form to master. This is best avoided for anyone developing their mediumship. Of course, it may simply happen as it did with me, during my first time at Plane Castle. I was undertaking an experiment called Human Pendulum when I started to shout *Get Out! Get Out!* at everyone, much to their panic and excitement. This is why it's really important to make sure that you have someone with you who can step in and help you if required. It needs to be someone you can trust and with whom you can be open with.

Maintain a diary of any connections that you experience. These can be complex and may take the form of dreams or visions. You may encounter spirit in your home or place of work. You may experience many coincidences. Jot them down and look for any emerging patterns. When working with spirit you need to trust in your instincts. Mediumship is very much about understanding your emotions and thoughts. You need to use all five senses and your intuitive perception.

Many people describe themselves as a *sensitive.*

This is a matter of disposition and choice. Personally, I don't use the term as I believe that we're all sensitive to one degree or another and that we're all mediums of a sort. Mediumship is not a binary condition but is rather a spectrum. So for some, they may be registering as a 1 (where they experience little – or seem to experience little) and a 10 (where they walk around and interact with the dead as they do the living). I'm probably around a 7 or an 8. I call this the Mediumship Probability Scale (you used it at the end of the Foreword – End of Chapter Reflection).

Don't be afraid to speak to spirit. Talk to them and ask them for guidance. Ask for signs that spirit is around you. Make sure you ask for a specific sign e.g. tell them what you want to see, hear or smell. That way, you'll recognise it when it comes. A common mistake is to assume that you've been given a sign. A white feather, for example may be a sign that you've had a visitor, or it could simply be that you've awakened in bed and you happen to have feather pillows. I always ask for abstract signs such as a flying pig or a car with white spots on it. The sign could come in the form of spoken word e.g. someone may say and *pigs might fly*, or it could be a photograph or cartoon on the TV.

Meditate! Look on *YouTube* for a 30 minute guided meditation. Any longer than that and you'll probably fall asleep. Find some quiet time and give it a go. Try to do this on a regular basis. I published a guided meditation on my *Facebook* page recently. Go and look for that and give it a go. You'll also find meditations on *Meeting Spirit Guides*, *Healing* and *Angels*.

Look for and attend a development circle or an awareness class. Make sure this is with a reputable medium who can also show you how to protect yourself by opening and closing to spirit. Some may charge for this and that's fine, but it should never bankrupt you. I would also be wary about training courses offered online (or even face-to-face) that promise you will become a medium upon successful completion. There is no such thing as a qualification in mediumship. There is such a thing as a qualification for holistic therapies such as Reiki or Hypnotherapy, but as far as being able to communicate with spirit and pass on messages, this is something that grows and develops within us. A training course may give you the tools that you need, but it won't give you the exposure and experience that moves you up that probability scale.

Don't be afraid to make mistakes. We are all human and contrary to belief, we're permitted to get things wrong now and again. Lord only knows I've made a few in my time and will likely make many more. You cannot control the actions or behaviours of other people and you could be telling them the names of loved ones in spirit, the conditions of passing and many other detailed information not readily available in the public domain, and yet they can be so closed in their mindset that the information you're giving them won't be assimilated. Sadly, there are some people out there who misunderstand mediumship. We have the TV to thank for that. It can be hard, but you need to try to forget about the people who call you a fake, a charlatan or a con artist. I've been called many things in the past. I remember being really upset once, not long after I'd started to appear on stage.

I was scrolling through Facebook and was messaging friends about a night out on the town when I happened to stumble upon someone's page. She was acquainted with me at school. I had not seen or spoken to her for around 16 years. Someone had shared a post on her timeline and had mentioned that I was doing a charity 'psychic' fundraiser. This person from my past had commented, to denounce my mediumship and to inform everyone willing to listen that she had known me at school and that she had never seen any 'special powers'. She went on to imply that I was a money making fraud.

I was both shocked and horrified.

Although I did know her from school, she was never in my immediate circle of friends. If she had been, she would have known that I was a bit weird and she would also have known about the whole 'lifeline' thing. I wasn't in the habit of going around telling everyone that I experienced spirit. Back then,

I was only a teenager and still trying to find myself. Anyway, I was doing this for charity. *How dare she!*

It also demonstrated an ignorance to the beliefs of other people. It's akin to telling anyone religious, with a strong faith, that they've got it all wrong and it's all nonsense. Unfortunately, religion has been a major cause of war in our past and it invokes strong emotions in people. This was exactly my reaction.

I had to step back after reading her comment, the temptation to say something smart to her was overwhelming. How dare she make out to know me, even though she had not seen or spoken to me for more than 16 years. I was incensed, but at the end of the day we should never feel the need to prove ourselves to other people. I had to learn that the hard way. Keep it in mind as you progress through your spiritual journey.

You'll also attract some negativity from those who are so religious that they cannot see past their own faith. Most, if not all religions, teach patience, respect and understanding. They teach a deep love for humanity that we should all abide to. So they should know better than to dismiss the beliefs of others. I encounter many people who don't subscribe to my ideas and that's fine. And when it comes to angels and demons, oh my goodness. Be prepared for that discussion. I was stalked by someone once, who kept calling me at work (I have no idea how he got my number) trying to recruit me in the 'coming war'. He wanted to know what side I was on, as mediumship could be *seen as God's work as equally as it could belong to the Devil*.

Of course, this is a nonsense and I've made my thoughts on the lighter and darker side of life very clear elsewhere in this book. But, one needs to remember that this is his belief and so it's often easier to accept that you're not going to change their mind. Challenge is good, but when one is so fixated, no amount of influence or evidence will make a difference. Accept them for who they are and move on. I'm not telling you this to put you off, but you do need to be aware that you'll attract unwanted attention. It would be poor of me to simply tell you that everything is amazing, when the reality is that spirituality and mediumship can be hard work. If I'd lived 500 years ago, I would most likely have been accused of witchcraft and burnt at the stake. Or worse. Luckily, those days are long gone, but the sentiment remains in the minds of some. It's also safe to admit that my family has been affected in a variety of ways. *Your dad's a ghost buster* and other comments to my children. People have stopped my wife in the street to ask her if they could arrange a meeting with me. I've even experienced occasions on the train, when people have stared at me and openly asked *are you that medium guy?*

END OF CHAPTER REFLECTION

If you wish to learn tarot (or any other card type) my advice is to throw away the book that accompanies them. This is someone else's interpretation of the cards and chances are, you'll never remember what they all mean. I started by only using the major arcana within tarot, it's less cards to think about. I had to try several decks before I found some that worked for me.

Try to focus on the card at hand instead of thinking about what it means, look to see if you're drawn to any particular part of the image, a colour or a number. Think about how this card makes you feel. Use your intuitive perception rather than your logic brain as that'll only take you so far. What images do you see in your mind? Are there any names or details that come to you? You're retraining your mind to work in a different way. This is how our conscious mind speaks to our soul. Don't be worried about getting things wrong. Just be honest and say it how you 'see' it.

PROPHECY

"I often have dreams which come true, or I think about something at random that later has significance."

The following extract is taken from two previous books that I'd written in recent years. *The Little Book of Prophecy* and *Intuitive Perception* outlined a number of predictions that I made between 2014 and 2016. They're no longer in print, but I can't write a book about mediumship without talking about dreams and predictions, so I thought I'd surface them here. I often have dreams which come true, or I think about something at random that later has significance. There have been many occasions when spirit has visited me in my sleep. Waking up to find them at the bottom of the bed watching over me, or glimpsing memories from their lives as they seek to communicate with me. Often, they visit over a number days or even weeks, or perhaps in visitation prior to a reading that I'm about to give. Every now and again they also appear to me when they wish me to pass on a message to someone that I know. This presents a challenge as I find it very difficult to read someone, or to pass on messages to someone that I know well. I tend to second guess the things that I experience and instead of trusting my intuitive perception, I start to make assumptions. This is exactly why I can't predict my own future, though there are times when something happens and I think to myself *I knew that was going to happen!*

Spirit find it easier to communicate in our dream state as our consciousness is altered and our brain waves typically move from Beta to Delta (the slowest brain waves) or even Theta, which tends to occur when we're in a trance like state such as in meditation. This, accentuated with rapid eye movement, loans itself to the ideal condition for spirit communication. It's not that different to the time that I participated in the experiment at Stirling University, where my head was strapped up to a computer so that my brainwaves could be mapped.

We can train our brains to act in this way - but it isn't an easy path to follow and it takes many years to build confidence. I suspect that when I'm actively working with spirit, my brainwave patterns may alter – making them more susceptible to human Wi-Fi. After 40 years, I'm still learning to say what I think, feel, see and hear. Although I've witnessed strange things for as long as I remember, only a few years ago did I gain a better understanding of what I was actually experiencing during my sleep.

I often receive requests to help with missing person cases. These are *really* tough and highly charged with emotion. As a general rule of thumb, I don't tend to get involved in active Police investigations. These are matters for the authorities and they're best placed to investigate. I've been involved in some cases in the past and once upon a time, I provided information from a dream that resulted in the discovery of human remains. But this isn't my niche and it isn't something that I plan to do again in the future. I once had a conversation with Noreen Renior, a psychic investigator based in the United States. Noreen has lectured at the FBI Academy in Quantico, Virginia and she's worked on more than 600 cases with law enforcement agencies across 38 States. I asked her how she managed the emotions of families and loved ones. I wanted to know how she worked, without providing them with false hope. She replied to me with a smile. *"Lee, we never give false hope. And we only give real hope when everything else seems lost."*

So, I now stick only to prophecy. And even then, I don't always put my thoughts into the public domain. In 2016, I made a number of predictions and I published these on *Facebook* at the time. These were based on dreams that I had been having and on experiences from meditation. I've listed them here in this chapter in their full form so that we may revisit them, together. So, what *exactly* did I see? War, famine, poverty and civil unrest featured highly, as did the destructive power of Mother Nature. Here is a narrative that describes what I foresaw. How much of it has come true and to what extent over the last few years, I'll let you determine. Perhaps some are still to occur.

ONE

The chariot offers little protection as a prominent Eastern leader is critically injured. The conspiracy that follows him will be his undoing, causing unrest as a star falls from the sky. This will cause war and unrest in surrounding nations. There is a connection to Russia.

TWO

The announcement of another royal pregnancy coincides with news of a royal passing. The circle of life is completed as one soul enters this earth plane and another rejoins the Higher Side of Life.

THREE

East and West forge new lines in the sand as China and Russia announce an economic union - this will coincide as India enters into a solidarity pact with Western nations and North Korea enters talks with the South. There will be broken promises of a new Euro-Asian Union.

FOUR

A major car manufacturer will seek liquidation or sale.

FIVE

A great storm of fire will threaten and partially destroy the Yellowstone ecosystem as human intervention fights against the explosive force of Mother Nature.

SIX

A love triangle emerges when a celebrity falls pregnant with another man's baby following an affair. All is not what it seems and this will dominate the papers for a few days.

SEVEN

A ship of the line will encounter trouble as it takes on water, one of a series of maritime concerns which includes the disappearance of a private yacht as it attempts to navigate troubled seas, with many people passing over in the water as they attempt to seek new life in another country.

EIGHT

Scientists will make a major breakthrough in our knowledge of cellular regeneration, which leads to potential new treatments for neurodegenerative conditions. This is linked to research on cloning, DNA (cancer research) and genetic engineering.

NINE

A great sword of light interferes with communications as we experience a solar flare, which affects satellites orbiting the planet. Mobile phone networks will be knocked out for a few hours and planes will be grounded. We will be warned about this in advance BUT it will not be as bad as feared. Expect a few hours of annoyance.

TEN

A cruise ship is attacked by pirates and takes some damage. This will be the first of two similar incidents within the space of a few days. The second will be an attack against a merchant navy vessel.

ELEVEN

A hot air balloon will crash land hitting the news headlines.

TWELVE

Darkness surrounds the passengers on a train as a tunnel collapse leaves them stranded underground for a few hours. Scientists will develop a new antibiotic, which begins a new era of drug development to tackle illness and disease. There is a running headline too - why we should eat cheese for good health!

THIRTEEN

Banking and global finance features strongly - the current landscape will change with several global super banks emerging at the same time as a reintroduction of localised building societies and civil trusts.

FOURTEEN

Expect a major revamp of mortgages and long term borrowing - though a theft of the financial kind will shake another bank at its roots when a vault is raided in a daring heist. There may also be a cyber-theft at the same time from another bank.

FIFTEEN

A light storm from the heavens turns our attention above as our technology loses orbit and lights up the sky.

SIXTEEN

News of a sunken ship beneath the oceans will accompany revelations of lost treasures as a wreck is found by chance.

SEVENTEEN

Alexandria and Atlantis will be the focus of discussion – have we found the mythical city?

EIGHTEEN

International attention is drawn to Peru as the global community notes the headlines of many newspapers. The forest comes alive.

NINETEEN

Missing flight MH370 will be found intact and on land. There will be no logical explanation as to how it arrived at its destination. Prayers go out to those missing in this modern day Mary Celeste. The voyage card features again as we see several maritime incidents and plane accidents.

TWENTY

We say goodbye to two popular and known male Scots as the circle of life completes. One triggers reruns of one of the most infamous film franchises created and the other a character that's Scotland personified through a political connection.

TWENTY ONE

Mother Nature features again as the Earth's magnetic field shifts. Something old, which has been quiet, is about to reawaken due to our interference and obsession of digging to the centre of the planet causing several earthquakes and many casualties. There are lessons to be learned about our existence and history - with newly discovered bacteria a catalyst for illness and new medicines. News of Ebola will hit western nations.

TWENTY TWO

A dark cloud hangs over a sporting event as a firearm is discharged into the crowd. A major terrorist attack will hit several countries simultaneously – this coincides with a significant cyber-attack, which disrupts the internet and telecommunications.

TWENTY THREE

There is an assassination attempt on a key politician who declares the war on terror as 'World War 3' with a shooting in France and a link to sun and a swimming pool of blood.

TWENTY FOUR

There will be a health scare for a religious icon - public events and private meetings to be cancelled as a result. Could The Pope require heart surgery?

TWENTY FIVE

An incident at a theme park leaves several people injured. An aviation collision as two airplanes collide whilst one is waiting to land.

TWENTY SIX

A major earthquake to hit The United States coastline, which will also bring flooding and destruction to property. Another series of terrorist incidents. Sadly, I do believe that the UK will be drawn into another armed conflict in Syria and surrounding nations as the war against ISIS takes on new forms. Expect a major revelation when a UK based cell and training centre is uncovered by intelligence services.

TWENTY SEVEN

Problems with milk – there will be a recall or issue with milk, as it appears a batch has become infected with bacteria.

TWENTY EIGHT

Yet more maritime and plane incidents – including a jet plane accident with major loss of life. I believe that a plane will come down in a major city of the world.

TWENTY NINE

NASA will reveal that it does believe life exists on other planets as it releases footage and image related to unexplained 'flying objects'.

THIRTY

A house of death will feature in the news as several bodies are discovered. This will coincide with headlines news on 'Jack the Ripper'.

THIRTY ONE

The news will feature young parents aged 9 and 13 respectively. They will have a little girl and will name her Faith.

Scientists will successfully implant a 'chip' into the human brain, which allows direct connection to bionic limbs.

THIRTY TWO

There will be an explosion of flame and heat in which a famous actor will pass over.

THIRTY THREE

There will be a major bridge collapse.

THIRTY FOUR

Expect a period of drought as water becomes scarce. I know – that's hard to believe, isn't it?!

THIRTY FIVE

We'll see news regarding a massive issue in a power station. This will lead to fire and to the loss of power in many homes. Liberation features, as news regarding a zoo hits the media. The freedom won by an escaped animal will be short lived as it is tracked down. This headline will coincide with the announcement that a woolly mammoth has been found frozen beneath the arctic ice cap, preserved and awaiting discovery by intrepid explorers. We'll see more news about the receding polar icecap and the rising sea levels.

THIRTY SIX

News of a child lost, will feature, with a major breakthrough and discovery regarding her fate. An arrest and further investigation will bring surprising revelations to the fore as the World looks on, wondering. We will see many cold cases reopened as the authorities begin to explore evidence not previously available to them. This will also lead to the revelation that there was a huge miscarriage of justice as someone infamous is pardoned for a crime that they did not commit.

THIRTY SEVEN

I am taken to Disney Land in America and to The Kennedy Space Centre. I hear whispers about Camp David and these may be symbolic of a connection between the President of the United States of America and the State of Florida, where I see a potential incident that will shake the political core.

Not all threats come from terror groups and domestic policies will not be liked by everyone.

THIRTY EIGHT

Sad news of a life lost will hit the headlines next year as someone drowns in a swimming pool accident. There is a connection to the UK and the possibility of a forced closure that will impact upon the holiday plans of many Brits.

THIRTY NINE

The media will be populated with a story about a child found living wild with animals. A modern day story of the Jungle Book, as journalists and investigators seek to identify the child and reunite them with their family.

FORTY

There will be several clashes of nations as their naval forces and aircraft clash; the downturn of commercial air travel will see a major holiday airline seeking liquidation towards the Autumn.

FORTY ONE

I am taken into a large church, possibly a Cathedral and as I walk inside, I am aware that this is an old building steeped in history. It has survived the Great Wars and many other events. I cannot help but feel there is a royal connection. The Peace card defines the environment but will be disturbed by rolling smoke, thin and wispy to begin with and then as thick as a blanket. I cannot see fire but I know it's there. All will be calm in the end but within a short space of time, there will be a number of ups and downs for all faiths. A religious or church connection?

FORTY TWO

The body card returns again as this time we will see news that scientists have made a breakthrough in designer drugs. This will be the start of a longer journey but new medicines designed for individuals and not the mass market will target illness and conditions more effectively than multiple medications offered at present. Stratified medicine features around Easter. Expect these to come at a price, though.

FORTY THREE

A trio of artistic influences presents itself in the media; a narrative of stolen artwork; a fire and a discovery of an old painting from a master. A Museum and Nazi Germany will all feature in the news with expensive paintings and drawings at the centre of the rhetoric. As we lose some pieces, others will be found in their place.

FORTY FOUR

I have already mentioned cloning in a previous advent and this one suggests that technology will advance in other ways too. I see big steps forward next year, in artificial intelligence, drone technology and computing power as scientists begin to merge biological matter with technology to produce new microprocessors. I also see a major incident involving a drone and possibly a collision with an aircraft.

FORTY FIVE

The Skills card takes me to football and there will be a few featured events next year. The first is financial ruin for a big club, with possibility of bankruptcy and the need for a big bailout. I am also shown a newspaper that contains a story about a famous player who will be tragically killed in a motor vehicle accident. This will be one of many events, as another player announces a terminal illness.

FORTY SIX

The Destruction card has been drawn again and this time I really do see some chaos. I am taken to North Korea as this isolated nation will feature heavily. A mass scale industrial disaster will cause significant loss of life - possibly as they lose containment over Nuclear material. Russia will feature around this situation as they continue to spread their military might around the Eastern side of the World. This coincides with talks with the US.

FORTY SEVEN

Synthetic fuel will pioneer travel as scientists begin to explore revolutionary new sources of power and combustion. Not only will we see news of newly manufactured sources to replace petroleum chemicals, but experimentation with micro fusion will begin in remote areas of the World as we seek alternatives to bio fuels and fossil energies. As the

Earth warms and the ice fields recede into the Oceans, we discover an ancient beast, buried beneath the frozen landscape for many years. Will this discovery unlock secrets from history?

FORTY EIGHT

Our future will bring political and economic unrest across the World, with major disruption in several countries and with riots in many European capitals. In these places, many people come together to show their anger towards political leaders. Other countries will leave the EU as it starts to break down and new alliances are formed. The UK and Australia form an economic pact. Within the UK, a new political party emerges and gains traction very quickly, proposing a new federal state system to devolve powers and finances locally. We will see massive change in the World as it seeks to rebalance - the first major world transition for 60 years.

FORTY NINE

Remember Dolly The Sheep? Next year will bring news that humanity has been playing God, yet again. We've produced another clone. This will coincide with news that we have the ability to clone a human being. Ethics and morals will be debated but medically, scientists will begin to explore stratified medicine, that is, using DNA to clone organs and tissue for operations. Although at the early stages, this will begin a new era for medical advancement. The running headline will also mention designer babies.

FIFTY

I am in some sort of shopping centre or mall. I hear music playing in the background and there are many people walking about. Although I do not see any threats, I am aware that I am not safe. I have the impression that armed men are close by. My impression is very much a hostage situation. I see yellow caps / hats on the ground and possibly a connection to the month of March.

FIFTY ONE

London Bridge is Falling Down! During the night, I had a dream that I was in London (again) and watching construction crews at work on this famous bridge. Expect news that there are some problems with the bridge and that it will need to go through some extensive repairs to put them right.

FIFTY TWO

A famous sportsman will be given the key to the City by the London Mayor. The stars and space feature quite a bit next year, as humanity explores its potential to reach for the heavens. Technology will take a giant leap forward as a new aircraft design reaches the upper atmosphere to travel the world, reducing travel time from A to B. We become more daring, as someone creates a new world record by jumping from orbit and a new planet will be discovered be an amateur astronomer. I am also taken into a research centre full of computers and there is a lot of excitement as scientists believe that they intercept signals from another world. Could we have alien contact? Or is it the sound of a dying star?

FIFTY THREE

I am taken to London. I can see the famous landmarks. The Bridge. The Tower. The Palace. There will be two explosions in two places. One involves a red bus and the number 23 features. This could be a date or other associated number. I also have a strong feeling that something is about to happen on or around Christmas, possibly with a building made of glass as when I look up at it, the glass is breaking and falling all around me in slow motion.

END OF CHAPTER REFLECTION

Our dreams can hold secrets that when considered, may provide us with insights into our life and into the world around us. Maintaining a dream diary can help you make sense of your subconscious thoughts.

1. Buy yourself a nice journal or a notebook that will only be used to record your dreams.
2. Make physical space for your diary. Think about where you'll keep it e.g. in a bedside drawer.
3. Try to record your dreams in the same way, so that the format is similar with each entry. Consider the context of the dream, who appeared in it, what did you/they do? Was the dream from your eyes or someone else's? How did it make you feel?
4. Look for patterns over a 7 day period and note anything that seems to be emerging. If there is a common theme, try looking on the internet or in a dream dictionary to discover the meaning or symbolism.

THE FUTURE

"I know that I need to trust in myself and in spirit more, and do and say the right things to the right person at the right time, so that's what I'm working on now."

So, what's next for me? That's a good question and I don't actually know the answer. At least not clearly. When we work with spirit, we find that we all have our own niche. That is, we have particular skills and ways of doing things. I may work in similar ways to other mediums, but there will be strong differences based on our upbringing, beliefs and even in the way that we work with spirit. This is why I've encouraged you to try different things and see where it takes you when developing your own spiritual awareness.

To quote Paloma Faith, you've got to *Make Your Own Kind Of Music*.

Likewise, we all have things we are well known for, or things that we *will do* and *won't do*. I know many excellent mediums who don't work on paranormal investigation and others who don't facilitate readings. You've got to do what you're 'assigned' to do by spirit. So you may *think* you want to read people, but you may *end up* healing or working with crystals.

I've been up on stage in the past and perhaps that's where I'm heading again. I enjoyed it at the time but I've never been one for passing on messages to an audience (apart from the odd impromptu message that I pass when I'm on an investigation). I think that's because I'm worried about what I might say and that I'll give away a family secret or say something inappropriate. People can be complicated and you'd be amazed at some of the things that I've told clients in the past. These things could not be mentioned in front of an audience. I always maintain confidence in what is said between myself and a client, unless I believe they pose a threat to themselves or to someone else and then I have a duty of care to inform the relevant authorities. I know that I need to trust in myself and in spirit more, and do and say the right things to the right person at the right time, so that's what I'm working on now. At the time

I'm writing this book, I'm planning to appear on stage for the first time in around four years. We'll see how that goes as it will determine what I do next.

During this lifetime, I have many lessons to learn and I've already outlined some of them in earlier chapters of this book. I'll seek to tackle those as they come along and as I become aware of what they are. That's some advice to you, in dealing with all situations in life. Ask yourself *What lesson have a I learned here? What worked well? What didn't work well? What would I do differently next time?* And last, but crucially, *How have my actions and behaviours impacted on the life of others?*

Remember to include thought and consideration to your immediate and indirect circle of influence. Our souls learn together as well as individually and our life is dependent on other people and the decisions that they make. That's what makes it interesting.

I'll also return to my writing. I want to write more fiction and complete the Silas series. I've given you some bonus material in the next chapter as an example of my fiction. It's not a million miles away from my thoughts and opinions on spirituality, the paranormal and splashed with an ounce of science fiction. I'm sure you'll recognise my style and interpretation around the spiritual aspects.

The 3am Club is a non-profit investigation team offering charity and public investigations across Scotland and the United Kingdom. Working with Linda, Helen and Lynda, together we investigate alleged paranormal activity from a spiritual perspective and we support the historic conservation of local and national landmarks, working discreetly and with respect to spirit and the property we are investigating. It's this aspect that I really enjoy as I firmly believe that we need to invest our time and energy into old buildings. We've lost so many over the years and we need to protect our heritage, so investigation and donations to their preservation are high on my agenda. I was a Friend of Sauchie Tower previously and I'm now a volunteer at Bannockburn House, so I'd like to give more of my time there.

I am *not* a ghost hunter. My aim is to investigate and educate people on aspects of spirituality and paranormal activity. I offer public events but unlike some mediums working with events companies, many of my investigations are private and are held in homes and places of work. I don't schedule investigations every month of the year and I offer a free service to anyone experiencing suspected paranormal activity. Working with The 3am Club is important to me. We established as a new group in June 2014 but our team are all experienced, having been part of other groups around the country. We decided to do this as we shared a common approach to investigation. We don't like the commercialisation of paranormal investigation for profit or gain. There are some great teams out there, but there are equally others who do not share our ethos. If you plan to attend an investigation, I'd advise that you do your research and make sure you're going to have a good time. You may not experience anything paranormal, but it's best to know that you'll be safe, looked after and that the event doesn't include more than thirty people crammed into two small rooms. For your information, I've included our terms and conditions at the end of this book. You should look for similar if attending an investigation as any reputable group will have something similar. They'll take health and safety seriously (you're working in the dark!) and your experience will be important to them. They'll also work with public liability and other insurances. If you don't see this advertised, ask before you buy tickets and you attend their investigation.

I don't see anything changing for me in the future around paranormal investigation. If anything, I may increase my activity with the possibility of undertaking investigations overseas. Likewise, I want to turn my attention to spiritual teaching and to the delivery of workshops. I'm a lifelong learner and I plan to enhance my study into the paranormal. I employ a scientific and evidenced based approach to investigation and I'm interested in psychical research, history, folklore and parapsychology. I once had the pleasure of meeting Steve Mera and Archie Lawrie, both well-known figures in the field of paranormal investigation. I found these conversations inspiring and through conversation with like-minded people, I find myself discovering new insights into how spirit works. Although the majority of my mediumship focuses on spirit and hauntings, I'm fascinated by UFOs and aliens. I do believe that there is life on other worlds (as explained in the chapter about the eternal soul) and this is something that I intend to explore further. Many believe that there is a firm connection between these areas of investigation. Oddly, when working as Senior Lecturer at the University of Glasgow, I also carried out some work looking at existential events and global catastrophic risk. I taught a course to third year undergraduate students called *Technology and Society*, which looked at the impact of technology on humanity. Technological determinism and social shaping is something that I'm grounded with academically and the potential for opportunity and threat from artificial intelligence and alien incursion is something that I'm already familiar with. Applying spirituality to my academic knowledge isn't such a big a leap as one may think. It's this philosophy that drives my fictional writing.

I've always been ambitious but I'm driven by a need to be the best that I can be. So I'll continue to do that, but keeping in mind my need for equilibrium. I do know that I'm ready for a rest, so I plan to take a sabbatical quite soon so that I can reflect my next steps in more detail. I need to take time away and reflect on my life as a spiritual medium and see where Harold guides me next.

Of course, I also need to spend time with my family. Each passing moment is as precious as the next and we can't afford to waste them. So these will be my final words to you in this manuscript. A personal message directly from me to you.

Regardless of what is thrown at you, you need to succeed despite of life. It's what you make it. Family, relationships with the souls around you and learning lessons in your lifetime are what matters the most.

I've never been one of those people who can *get their sh*t together* quickly or one of those people *where no f**ks are given,* but that doesn't mean I don't try. Life is much simpler if we concentrate our effort on the important things and we attempt to leave everything else behind.

I'll see you soon and I hope my memoirs have helped you in some way, but wherever you are on your journey, good luck!

TERMINOLOGY

I've used a variety of terms throughout this book. Here, I've pulled them together for you, and added in a few more for good measure. It's not a complete A-Z but it's a good start.

Agent A living person who is the focus of spirit activity. For example, this could be you or it could be a child.

Angel A spiritual being ordained by the Higher Side of Life that seeks to bring peace and balance to all on the Earth Plane.

Anomaly An unusual event that does not follow a normal rule that cannot be explained by current scientific theories.

Apparition An image of a person that materialises even though a physical body is not present. This could be interpreted as a *Ghost*.

Astral The spiritual body that a person occupies during an out-of-body experience. Sometimes spirit are referred to as *Astrals* or *Astral Beings*.

Astral Plane A world that is believed to exist above our physical world. This is opposite to the *Earth Plane*. Also known as The Higher Side of Life or what some would regard as Heaven.

Astral Projection When the soul leaves the body through a voluntary act.

Astrology The theory and practice of interpreting the positions and aspects of celestial bodies in the belief that they have an influence on the course of natural earthly occurrences and human affairs.

Aura Invisible emanation of electromagnetic energy that surrounds a person or thing; often thought to reflect a person's personality, health or emotional state.

Automatic Writing This method of obtaining information from spirit is used by mediums when spirit takes control over pen and paper.

Banshee A wailing spirit or "death omen" that is said to appear prior to someone passing over to the Higher Side of Life.

Case Study An investigation into an individual subject or event.

Channeling When spirit energy interacts with a person and they take on characteristics such as voice, movement or emotion.

Clairalience Ability to smell or experience odour outside the range of normal olfactory perception.

Clairaudience Ability to hear spirit talk.

Clairgustance Ability to perceive or experience taste without putting anything in the mouth.

Clairsentience Ability to perceive or experience the emotions of others without the use of the normal five physical senses.

Clairvoyance An acute insight or perceptiveness that enables one to see objects or events that cannot be perceived by the senses; comes in the form of mental imagery such as signs and symbols.

Control Procedure in paranormal psychology which ensures that the experiment is conducted in a standard fashion so that results will not be influenced by any extraneous factors.

Control Group Group of outside subjects whose performance or abilities are compared with the experimental subjects. Often used in experiments to establish a baseline.

Déjà vu An impression or dull familiarity of having seen or experienced something before. This is a common experience for someone undergoing a spiritual awakening.

Demon An inferior deity recognised by all religions but known by differing names and physical descriptions; often spoken of in religious text as pure evil; capable of human possession, possessed of inhuman strength, malevolent and destructive. Documented cases of demons are extremely rare.

Direct Voice Phenomenon (DVP) An auditory "spirit" voice that is spoken directly to the sitters at a séance.

Distraction Technique Used to aide communication with spirit e.g. tarot cards, crystal balls or sketching.

Doppelganger An exact spirit double or mirror image of a person which is considered to be very negative.

Dowsing Rod Simple tool of metal or wood used to locate water, lost objects, energy fields or in spirit communication. Established use has been known for centuries but carries little or no weight within current science.

Earthbound Term referring to a ghost or spirit that was unable to cross over to the other side at the time of death and is therefore stuck in this physical *Earth Plane*. Also known as grounded spirit.

Earth Plane A world that is believed to exist around us when we are in physical form. This is opposite to the *Astral Plane*.

Ectoplasm An immaterial or ethereal substance associated with spirit manifestations. Often photographed as fog-like mist, white masses or vortexes.

Electromagnetic Field (EMF) Energy field surrounding all things, both natural and man-made.

Electromagnetic Field (EMF) Detector – (See Magnetometer)

Electronic Voice Phenomenon (EVP) Voices and sounds from spirit that are captured and recorded on magnetic tape or by digital means.

Elementals Term commonly referring to natural spirits that have never taken human form.

Entity Anything that has a separate, distinct existence, though not necessarily material in nature. Entities are often referred to as *Demons* and vice versa.

Extra Sensory Perception (ESP) Communication or perception by means other than the normal five physical senses. Also known as the *sixth sense* or *intuitive perception*.

Exorcism The banishment of an entity or entities (spirits, ghosts, demons) that are thought to possess or haunt a location or human being or animal. The ritual, which can be religious in nature, is conducted by an exorcist who will call upon a Higher Power to cast away any evil forces that may be present.

Frank's Box A device which some believe allow real-time communication with spirit; works by continuously scanning AM and FM radio frequencies from which broadcast syllables or words are used by an entity to speak. Often called a ghost box.

Ghost Generic term referring to a form of apparition or supernatural entity; typically the visual appearance of a deceased human spirit or a replay from the past. Ghosts are not intelligent spirit interactions and they are not aware of our presence on this Earth Plane.

Ghost Hunt Carefully controlled research project in which various methods and equipment are used to investigate reports of ghosts and hauntings. Differs from an investigation in that no intervention of the research team has been requested. This is not a term that I like to use.

Ghoul Demonic or parasitic entity that feeds upon living humans.

Hallucination Vivid perception of sights and/or sounds that are not physically present. Usually associated with an altered state of consciousness induced by alcohol, drugs, illness or psychological instability.

Haunting Reoccurring ghostly phenomena that returns to a location where no one is physically present. Ghosts generally haunt places and not people. (See Intelligent and Residual Haunting).

Hellhound Spectral death omen in the form of a ghostly dog. I see these as elemental energies.

Hypnosis Technique that induces a sleep-like state in which the subject acts only on external suggestion. This is often used for past life regression.

Illusion A perception between what is perceived and what is reality.

Infra-red Camera (IR Camera) Camera with incorporated infra-red technology that allows photography or filming in low light conditions. Sometimes referred to as a night vision camera.

Infra-red non-contact thermometer (IR Thermometer) Instrument with incorporated infra-red technology that allows the measurement of both ambient and surface temperatures without physically being in contact. Extreme and rapid temperature change is believed to be an indicator of paranormal activity.

Instrumental Transcommunication (ITC) Term used to describe the many ways unexpected spirit voices can be collected through modern technological methods. Includes EVP, white noise, video frequency feedback.

Intelligent Haunting Where there is interaction on the Earth Plane with intelligent spirit.

Interaction when intelligent spirit use energy to make themselves known to us.

Intuitive Perception the ability to use all senses and interact with spirit through meaningful communication. Sometime sreferred to as the sixth sense

Investigation - Carefully controlled research project in which various methods and equipment are used to seek confirmation of reports of ghosts or hauntings. Differs from a ghost hunt in that the research team was requested to intervene.

K-II Meter - (See Magnetometer)

Levitation – To lift or raise a physical object in apparent defiance of gravity.

Magnetometer (EMF meter, Gaussmeter) Instrument for measuring the magnitude and direction of a magnetic field; typically used by paranormal researchers to detect spiritual energy.

Materialisation When spirit or a ghost begins to take form from thin air. See *apparition*.

Medium Someone who professes to be able communicate with spirits of the dead and living human beings.

Mist An anomaly that appears to manifest from spirit.

Near Death Experience (NDE) Event that is reported by people who clinically die, or come close to actual death and are revived. These often include encounters with spirit guides, seeing dead relatives or friends, out-of-body experiences (OBE), or a moment of decision where they are able to decide or are told to turn back.

Orb Most commonly photographed anomaly that theoretically represents the "spirit" of a deceased person. Often appears as a ball of light on film though in some cases they are not seen at the time of the photo. Differing characteristics include size, color, density, shape, motion and flexibility. Since there are many reasonable causes for their origin (dust, moisture, insects, lens reflection, etc.) orbs remain highly controversial.

Ouija Board A pre-printed board with letters, numerals, and words used to receive spirit communications. Typically a planchette, a triangular or heart-shaped pointer, or an upside down glass is employed to spell out words or messages and point out numbers or letters. Many believe the controversial board is a gateway allowing negative entities into the physical plane while others believe it no more harmful than any other board game. Also referred to as a spirit board.

Out-of-body experience (OBE) Sensation or experience in which one's self or spirit travels to a different location other than their physical body.

Paranormal Term referring to something that is beyond the range of normal human experience or scientific explanation.

Parapsychology The study of the evidence for psychological phenomena that are inexplicable by science.

Pareidolia Psychological phenomena whereby random and vague stimuli are perceived as being significant. Common examples include finding images of animals or faces in clouds.

Phantom Something that is seen, heard and/or sensed, but has no physical reality (See Ghost).

Poltergeist Non-human entity which literally means "noisy ghost" but is usually more malicious and destructive than spirit. Traditional poltergeist activities are thumping and banging, levitation or movement of objects, stone throwing and starting fires. It is thought that poltergeist activity in some instances may be brought on subconsciously by an adolescent, females under the age of 25 or by individuals under extreme emotional duress. Documented cases of poltergeists are relatively few.

Precognition or Prophecy Ability to predict or have knowledge of an event in advance of its occurrence, especially by extrasensory perception.

Psychic Term used to describe a person who has above average ESP abilities or paranormal powers; term used to describe forces of a paranormal nature.

Psychic Magnetism Where one feels a pull or the need to go to a specific place without thinking about it. Occasionally, it works in reverse e.g. we think about someone and then receive a message from them.

Psychometry The ability or art of divining information about people or events associated with an object solely by touching or being near to it.

Reading Session during which a medium or psychic reveals information to a sitter through various means such as astrology, palmistry, tarot cards or by spiritual means.

Reciprocal Apparition Extremely rare type of spirit phenomenon in which both a living person and spirit are able to see and respond to each other.

Reflection When the soul leaves the physical body and makes the transition to the Higher Side of Life (or the Astral Plane) it enters into reflection on the life that it has just had – to learn the lessons taught.

Remote Viewing Used by some psychics, a procedure in which the percipient or psychic attempts to become physically aware of the experience of an agent who is at a distant, unknown location through ESP.

Residual Haunting Case in which an event or scene is re-enacted and is not affected by any external influences. Typically, ghostly activity may be experienced.

Retrocognition Experience in which a person finds themselves in the past and is able to see and experience events of which they had no prior knowledge.

Séance Meeting or gathering of people, usually lead by a medium, to receive spiritualistic messages, manifestations of and/or communication with the dead.

Sensitive Term referring to persons who possess extrasensory talents. Another way to describe a medium.

Shadow People Shadow-like spirit that are often caught from the corner of the eye.

Sleep Paralysis Form of paralysis often striking as a person falls asleep, awakens or moves into or out of the rapid-eye movement (REM) stage of sleep.

Spiritualism The belief system that the dead are able to communicate with the living, most often through an intermediary or medium. This is also a religious stance often confused with Buddhism or a natural and benign way of thinking.

Stigmata Unexplained bodily marks, sores, or sensations of pain corresponding in location to the crucifixion wounds of Christ.

Supernatural Of or relating to existence outside the natural world. As opposed to paranormal, the term "supernatural" often connotes divine or demonic intervention.

Trance A hypnotic, cataleptic, or ecstatic state in which one becomes detached from their physical surroundings. This is often found in deep meditation or relaxation.

Tunnelling A technique used to visualise spirit in the mind.

Vortex An anomaly that appears as a funnel or rope-like image in photographs. Sometimes thought to represent ghosts, collections of orbs or gateways which travel to a wormhole in time-space, there is no substantial scientific evidence to support any of these theories. Also referred to as a portal.

White Noise An acoustical or electrical noise of which the intensity is the same at all frequencies within a given band.

BONUS MATERIAL

The following is an extract from my fictional novel, Silas Awakening. This is due for republication later in 2020.

Silas is an 18 year old living in a dystopian universe, haunted by a vast interstellar war. With no place to call home, he travels from one star system to the next, exploring abandoned ships, space stations and citadels as he unwittingly begins to unlock the secrets of his past. From a young age, Silas realised that he had the ability to see the darkness in people. He doesn't know where this power comes from, nor does he understand the experiences that life throws at him. Harnessing his intuition and his profound sense of right and wrong, he believes that his mission is simple. To save the future of all humanity. Or to die trying.

*   *   *

Before the elements, there was nothing. The Cosmos is vast, dense and formed of a single point of energy. It is both the beginning and the end. There is expansion. Thus created from the primordial singularity, as cosmic rays erupted into infinity, stars grew shedding light onto the millions of distant bodies gathered around the universe. For millennia, the source assembled its intelligence and watched quietly the slow passage of time. Waiting in the shadows for ages, it suddenly realises that the universe is changing. The primordial energies that formed its intelligence begin to whisper through the dark. It moves from one world to the next, searching for a companion. It exists yet it has no shape or form. Alone, it is self-aware and vast.

Finally, it finds what it is looking for. A world that can support physical life. Desperate to find corporeal form, the source divides its intelligence and sends forth ambassadors, pure energy taking physical form on a world grounded by life. This is not the first time it has done this, for it already gathers knowledge and experience from a world adorned with crystalline structures, where two suns orbit at distance and where millions of souls continue to live and to die. Here, on this new world it calls Earth, as the source grants self-will and a thirst to learn and grow, it's amused as the ambassadors it calls humans, evolve.

*   *   *

I didn't care much for the wind, but I actually liked the rain. It not only cleaned the City, but is also meant that some of the people best avoided would be indoors. They haunted the street corners and the alleyways, injecting poison into the world like dirty liquid spurting from a syringe. I can hear sirens in the distance and shuttles hurried overhead, carrying their wary passengers to their next destination.

Some regarded the Commonwealth with awe, but even at the tender age of ten years, I knew better. The modern age had spiraled down into the tenth level of hell and the gates had been well and truly opened. As always, our inhumanity was shunned in public, well at least by the elites in their ivory towers, looking down on the alien world below. Privately, it was worshipped by people as they gathered around the telecom channels to watch the latest news, dominated by loss of life on another distant planet, charred bodies scattered about another City, not that dissimilar from the one in which I stood.

A voice at my back and I remembered where I was. Not everyone had hurried indoors. Some remained, unperturbed by the poor weather.

"Go on, mate. Take it. It's on the house." The croaking voice of a short man came from the shadows of a deserted alley. I knew instantly who it was. I didn't move, frozen by sheer determination. Instead, I let my head drop to the side and tried to look Benny in the eye, which was difficult given that they both peered in different directions, moving independently of each other.

"I don't take the stuff, Benny. I told you, I'm clean." I said, firmly.

Benny glanced about nervously. Confident that no one was watching, he forced his eyes into a single, united gaze, his voice menacing. "You've been listening to them holy rollers, you have. Badmouthing the Saturn," he waved the fragment of Saturn at me as if it were precious quartz dug out from a long forgotten mine, instead of the lump of crap that it was.

I shook my head. "You've not been listening. I've seen people waste away with that. That's your ticket to power, not mine."

Benny shifted uneasily. I needed to be careful. He was as dangerous as he was stupid. "You'd better watch that mouth, boy," he moved towards me. "Or you may not be around tomorrow."

Now it was my turn to feel uneasy. Benny slipped the drug back into his pocket and with his other hand, he reached out to grab my arm. Despite my jacket, as his hand made contact with me, I felt something that I'd never experienced before. A chill that started on the nape of my neck, it continued down my spine and my whole body was cold in an instant. The street disappeared behind us and instead, I found myself in some sort of hotel room. Benny was there, younger and sharper. He was clean-shaven and fresh. I looked on as he argued with another man that I had never seen before. Benny reached beneath his coat and withdrew an energy rod and I felt like I was inside a movie. There was a struggle and a few seconds later, the stranger dropped to the floor, his body twitching in the throes of death.

"What's wrong with you, boy?" Benny's voice startled me. I was back in the street. The whole episode lasted only for a few seconds, but it was long enough for Benny to notice that I had phased out.

Trembling, I stepped back from him and let his hand drop away from my arm. I knew that he wasn't a good person, but somehow I also knew that he was a killer. Now, as I looked back at him, I saw something that I had not noticed before. His heart was black and his soul was tainted. I couldn't actually *see* his heart, but through instinct, I *knew* it to be true.

"Your heart is black." I said to him, as a matter of fact. The words slipped out from my mouth before I realised what I was saying. I had no idea where they had come from, but it felt as though someone else had said them.

Benny regarded me with suspicion and then he started to laugh. It was not a pleasant laugh. "Oh, that's brilliant," he continued to chuckle, his smile exposing missing teeth and a rotten world beyond.

"You sure you've not been on the Saturn? You are one weird kid, you know that?"

I had to get in good with him again. I wasn't sure what had just happened to me, but it left me unnerved and shaken. "You know me, I'm up for anything," I said, gripping my stomach. "But I'm not feeling well. I'm sick."

It wasn't exactly a lie. I did feel sick. My head was spinning and my heart pounded against my ribs like a beating drum ready to explode onto a stage. He eyed me again, but this time his united gaze was lost and his face softened.

"Aye, well. Get lost then. And tell your friends to come visit old Benny."

I nodded and as I turned away from him, I told him that I would, though I had no intention of doing such a thing. Now that the storm was over, people had gathered along the street, returning to their business. Now fifty meters away, I turned to see him still watching me. He shouted something, but I was too far away to hear him clearly.

Quietly, efficiently, I slipped into the crowd.

SILAS WILL RETURN IN AUGUST 2020

TERMS AND CONDITIONS

The following terms and conditions are set out clearly on my website. They equally apply to all aspects of my work as a spiritual medium, however the content here is focused around paranormal investigation. I encourage anyone attending an investigation to ensure that the team they go with has a similar operating culture.

Our events are not recommended for those with a fear of the dark, confined spaces or of a nervous disposition. We recommend warm clothing and sensible footwear be worn. By purchasing your tickets you confirm that you have read and agree to the Terms & Conditions. Please bring a torch, a snack and a drink. Areas investigated may vary subject to weather, restoration work or safety restrictions. Please be aware that the event may be filmed or photographed. Upon making payment, you, the client, confirm that you have read and agree to abide by these terms and conditions as set out below.

1. Ticket holders must be over 18 years of age. Proof of age may be required should you appear to be under the age of 18 years. Anyone unable to prove their age may be refused entry; in such circumstances no refunds will be made.

2. Anyone suspected of being under the influence of alcohol or other substances will not be permitted to enter or to remain on site and will be asked to leave the premises immediately, in such circumstances no refund will be made.

3. You are required to act in a sensible manner throughout the event and not cause harm or damage to other attendees, representatives or the fabric of any part of the venue. Anyone failing to do so will be asked to leave immediately, in such circumstances no refund will be made.

4. We reserve the right to refuse admission to any person or persons. Any person or persons who feel they have been refused admission unjustly can

request us to provide written reasons by making a request in writing to us within 7 days of the event.

5. We will not be liable for any loss of or damage to any equipment or belongings of participants during and after the event. Any property left unattended within the venue or its associated buildings and areas (including the car park) are left entirely at the owners risk.

6. Where any event or activity due to take place wholly or partially in the open air is affected by weather conditions which make that part of the event or activity dangerous or presents an unacceptable level of risk of harm to either tickets holders or our representatives then we reserve the right to alter or substitute that part of the programme without notice.

7. Paranormal investigations are conducted by The 3am Club and no responsibility for any emotional, physical or other upset brought on as a result of participating in the event is accepted.

8. We reserve the right to change, add, or amend to these terms and conditions at any time. We also reserve the right to change, add and amend any part of the event at any time without notice.

9. We do not normally supply refreshments throughout the period of the event. You will need to bring your own snack and drink. If we offer refreshments, we will inform you in advance.

10. The event may be filmed or photographed by us for our use and you agree that this may be included in promotional videos including on the internet. Should you not wish to be included, please inform a team member immediately upon arrival on site. You further understand that any photographic or film footage you provide to us either during or after the event may be subject to use in any promotional material by us.

11. Tickets are non-refundable and valid only for the event shown on the ticket.

12. All participants must follow the instructions given to them by our team at all times. This includes any local rules set out by the location manager or the venue representative.

13. Anyone with a medical condition (Heart, Blood Pressure etc.) should seek advice before attending. We do not permit anyone who is or thinks that they are pregnant to take part in our activities.

14. You agree that paranormal events operated by The 3am Club are classed as alternative entertainment and are solely for public entertainment purposes only. We make no guarantee regarding the validity of the supposed paranormal activity associated with our locations or information, obtained from any of our sensitives, psychics, mediums, investigators or volunteers. No perceived opinions, information, advice or comments made by any of our volunteers, guests, employees, sensitives, psychics or mediums should be interpreted as factual or actual.

Although we attempt to create atmosphere, The 3am Club does not set up any tricks in advance nor do we create false experiences. We are a legitimate spiritual research and investigation team and we act with honesty and integrity. We ask that our guests behave in the same way. Anyone caught faking paranormal activity will be asked to leave.

Connect with Lee Dunn

Facebook @LeeDunnMedium

www.the3amclub.uk

My disclaimer: Even though I take my mediumship seriously, I must make it clear that at this time, society only accepts it as a form of entertainment. This saddens me, but I understand why that's the case. Please consider any life changing decisions with care and always seek professional advice in matters of health and finance. Some of the names within this book have been altered. A special thanks to those who have allowed me to use their names and/or their stories. You're all amazing.

I've been careful not to make this book too academic. Much of the information comes from my own mind, however I have used some citations and quotes from *Wikipedia* in support of my arguments and ideas. Where possible, I have attributed content to the copyright owner.

NOTES

NOTES

NOTES

ACKNOWLEDGEMENTS

This book wouldn't have been possible without support from my family and friends. My life has been an interesting one and I still have much to learn. Spirit is constant for me and although I'm beginning to understand the truth about mediumship and the meaning of life, and although I do my best to teach others, this is a personal journey for me, too.

I want to thank my wife, Claire. She needs to put up with our spiritual visitors during the night and with my frequent toing's and going's from the house. Of course, my children inspire me and they motivate me to be the best human being that I can be. Role modelling is important. I love them very much.

I want to thank Linda, Helen and Lynda for their support and encouragement and for the laughs that we have along the way. I want to thank Caroline and Alan, dear friends of mine who have helped me considerably over the last few years.

I'd like to express my thanks to all those who believe in me and have faith that our souls have met for a reason, and that we can learn from each other along the way. Life places us in the path of another when we need them. I've met some wonderful mediums and investigators over the years. My former teacher, Georgina and others mentioned (directly or indirectly) have all contributed to the person that I am, today.

Last, I want to thank you for buying my book and for taking the time to read it. I take comfort and pride from the knowledge that my memoirs have helped you in some way. The writing of this book has allowed me to reflect on the person that I am, and the journey that I made from being a weird kid and teenager into adulthood (I'm probably still a bit weird). I'd love to hear from you. Connect with me via my *Facebook* page and let me know if I've done or said anything to help you or to motivate you on your spiritual journey. I don't set out to teach people how to become a medium, but I suspect that some of my experiences may resonate with you and that in reading my story, you feel the time is now right to work with spirit.

Printed in Great Britain
by Amazon